AFTER WESLEY

A STUDY OF THE SOCIAL AND POLITICAL INFLUENCE OF
METHODISM IN THE MIDDLE PERIOD (1791–1849)

AFTER WESLEY

A Study of the Social and Political Influence of Methodism in the Middle Period (1791–1849)

By

MALDWYN EDWARDS

M.A. (Wales), M.A. (Cantab.), Ph.D. (London)

Author of
John Wesley and the Eighteenth Century, &c. &c.

WIPF & STOCK · Eugene, Oregon

Wipf and Stock Publishers
199 W 8th Ave, Suite 3
Eugene, OR 97401

After Welsey
A Study of the Social and Political Influence of
Methodism in the Middle Period (1791 - 1849)
By Edwards, Maldwyn
ISBN 13: 978-1-62564-277-6
Publication date 8/15/2013
Previously published by Epworth, 1935

To
JILL
A GREAT LOVER OF JOHN WESLEY
AND A KEEN STUDENT OF THE HISTORY
OF THE PEOPLE CALLED METHODISTS

CONTENTS

Preface — 11

PART I
THE POLITICAL THOUGHT OF METHODISM IN THE PERIOD

CHAP.
I. The Dominant Toryism of Methodism — 15
II. The Underlying Liberalism — 38

PART II
METHODISM AND THE EVENTS OF THE PERIOD

I. The Agitation Against Slavery — 63
II. Sidmouth's Bill, 1811 — 75

PART III
METHODISM AND THE MOVEMENTS OF THE PERIOD

I. The Industrial Revolution — 85
II. Education — 100
III. Roman Catholic Relief — 110
IV. Humanitarianism — 116

PART IV
METHODISM AND THE SOCIAL LIFE OF THE DAY

I. Methodism and the Social Life of the Day — 127

PART V
THE RANGE OF METHODIST INFLUENCE

I. The Napoleonic Period — 141
II. Jabez Bunting: The Significance of his Career — 151

CONTENTS

APPENDIX I

TABLE TO SHOW THE INCREASE OF METHODISM BETWEEN 1789 AND 1815 163

APPENDIX II

DIRECTIONS FOR CONGREGATIONAL SINGING 172

BIBLIOGRAPHY

LIST OF NEWSPAPERS AND PERIODICALS 173
LIST OF CONTEMPORARY SOURCES 174
ANONYMOUS 181
COLLECTED PAMPHLETS AND TRACTS 183
LIST OF GENERAL WORKS 184
INDEX 189

PREFACE

THE study of the social and political influence of Methodism which I began in the book *John Wesley and the Eighteenth Century*, is continued in this present volume. The study has been completed in a third book, by examining the part played by Methodism in public affairs since the death of Jabez Bunting.

So far as I know, there is no book which covers the same ground as this one. The period has in fact suffered neglect because of the greater interest and importance of the days of Wesley. The histories of Methodism, which are the only books that have dealt with this middle period, have discussed mainly the growth of organization, and the various secessions from the parent society.

Yet this book would have no justification were it not that Methodism in these years exercised a vital influence on the social and political life of the day. In particular, it is not generally recognized that Methodism played an important part in the abolition of the Slave Trade and of slavery itself. The assistance Methodism gave to the elementary education of poor children through the institution of Sunday Schools has never been fully appreciated. Writers have pointed out the inability of Methodism to grasp the opportunity of the Industrial Revolution. The Hammonds in their notable books on this period have shown the lack of sympathy which official Methodism showed with the aspirations of the workers. In this book I have attempted to state the positive contribution Methodism was able to make to the new order by its philosophy of wealth. The relation of Methodists and Evangelicals was not so close as people generally imagine, and yet, as I have set myself to show, Methodism had a real share in the humanitarian enterprises of the early nineteenth century. The intransigent attitude of Methodists towards Roman Catholic relief, the menace of Sidmouth's Bill, and the relation of Methodists to the customs and habits of the age are other points I have discussed.

They are all, I think, subjects which needed further investigation, and they must constitute my reasons for writing a further book on Methodism. The main argument of the book has been to show the Toryism of Methodism at the beginning of this period and the ways in which it was made evident. As the period came near to its close, the Liberalism which had always been present grew more powerful. When Bunting retired the tide of Liberalism was flowing strongly. Methodism no longer sought friendship with the Church and the landed classes, but with Nonconformity and the middle classes which had been created by the Industrial Revolution.

The book is an expansion of the thesis which was presented to the University of London for the degree of Doctor of Philosophy. I have omitted the chapter on the French Revolution, because some of the points raised had already been discussed in my previous book. The last chapter is completely new, and short additions have been made to the thesis in other places. I have tried earnestly to avoid any overlapping with the first book on John Wesley. This is not wholly possible, since there is no rigid division between the two periods, but if at any point there is repetition, I think it will be found that the matter is discussed afresh and presented in a different way.

I wish to acknowledge with gratitude the help given by the Rev. F. F. Bretherton and by Dr. Henry Bett who read the book and made some wise suggestions. I am also greatly indebted to Professor Norman Sykes, whose generous encouragement led me to expand the thesis with a view to its ultimate publication.

Miss Alice Thompson has proved a most capable and conscientious typist. She has taken immense pains over her work, and her efficiency has made my task much lighter. My wife has assisted in the preparation of the Index, but that is the least of her services. She has read the book in typescript, and has shown constant interest in the preparation and writing of it.

MALDWYN EDWARDS.

PART I
THE POLITICAL THOUGHT OF METHODISM IN THE PERIOD

CHAPTER I

THE DOMINANT TORYISM OF METHODISM

JOHN WESLEY died in 1791, but it would be wrong to regard that year as the end of one period and the beginning of another. His death inevitably left a gap in leadership, and it left acute problems of administration to be settled. There were some who wanted the Conference of Preachers to take his place and use his authority. There were others, especially the wealthy trustees of many chapels, who demanded complete conformity to the Church of England. They would not tolerate the observance of the Sacrament of the Lord's Supper in Methodist chapels, nor the holding of Methodist services in the hours for Church worship. A third section desired a complete separation from the Church of England. They desired the Ordinances at the hands of their own ministers: they claimed freedom to worship at hours most convenient to the congregation and they wanted the co-operation of laymen with the preachers in the administration of Methodist Societies.

Apart from these problems of government, Methodism was not seriously disturbed by the passing of John Wesley. The religious and political thought of the Society remained unaffected. This is a remarkable tribute to the influence Wesley exerted over the whole Methodist Society. He had a genius for organization. Hearers were gathered into Societies, and visited by travelling preachers.

In time local Societies were linked together in Circuits; the Circuits were grouped in Districts,[1] and once a year there met together a Conference of Preachers who legislated for all the Societies. This system has been still further developed and perfected, but even in the eighteenth century it was capable of consolidating and unifying the activities of Wesley and his preachers throughout the land. This made it more easy for his ideas to be propagated and his decisions enforced. He had forged an instrument which he could use effectively, even though his adherents multiplied with such rapidity.

Wesley was almost eighty-eight years of age when he died. This perhaps is more illuminating than any other fact. It meant that the

[1] Districts were formed in the Conference after Wesley's death (1791).

Methodism he had founded and organized, he was able to direct for a long period. His ideas, indeed, had become so generally accepted by Methodists, that his death merely meant a change in leadership. It brought no change in the political and religious philosophy of Methodism. As early as 1776 the writer of a tract, called 'Political Empiricism,' had said 'many of your deluded followers have blind faith in your political as well as your theological creeds.' The truth of that statement had become even more evident by the year 1791. Crabbe put the matter succinctly when he wrote:

> All innovation they with dread decline,
> Their John the Elder was the John divine.

The political thought of Methodism at Wesley's death was therefore strongly conservative. That was inevitable since Wesley was so staunch a Tory. His political tenets were as clearly defined as his theological beliefs. He was brought up in a Tory and High Church family. Samuel Wesley, his father, had been educated at a Dissenting Academy, but had chosen to enter the Established Church. In speech and writing he showed warm attachment to the King and Constitution. Susanna Wesley, his mother, was able at thirteen years of age to weigh the arguments for Church or Dissent and become a convinced Anglican. The sharpest dispute of her married life arose because of her loyalty to the exiled Stuarts. The Toryism into which John was baptized, was reinforced by his residence at Oxford; of his early education at Charterhouse we know practically nothing.

In the seventeenth century Oxford had impoverished itself in supporting the cause of Charles I, and it was to Oxford that Charles II summoned Parliament when he was faced with the menace of the country party.

From the University in 1683 came the remarkable declaration which denied that civil authority was derived ultimately from the people, and which declared that there would be no compact between the King and his subjects. When John Wesley came to Oxford half a century later, he found there was the same loyalty to Church and State. The spread of Jacobitism had been checked by the stubborn determination of the Old Pretender to remain a Catholic. In consequence, Wesley found at Oxford an attitude to politics and religion which corresponded to his own.

He was by temperament unable easily to brook opposition or

THE DOMINANT TORYISM OF METHODISM

delegate his powers. He had no faith in the people's capacity for government, and it never occurred to him that they ought to be represented at Conference. Even the preachers who came were merely present in an advisory capacity. A letter was published in Dublin in 1777 with the title 'Reasons for leaving the Methodist Society,' and the contention of the writer was that the Methodist people were subordinated to the despotism of Conference, and the whole system was subversive of Christian liberty. When Benson asked Hopper if he should publish his sermons, Hopper replied: '. . . You know how we are circumstanced. If Mr. Wesley only speaks a word against them or gives a frown, that is enough. Thousands will neither buy, see, nor read them.'

Fletcher writing to Benson said: 'I have read this week in the *Minutes of Conference* a clause which enacts that whoever prints or publishes without Mr. Wesley's consent is to be cut off from the Connexion. I hope you have not overlooked the article.' It is not then a matter for surprise that Wesley accepted without question the rule of an aristocracy whose power was derived not from the people but from their money or their land. He was temperamentally fitted to understand the Toryism of his day, for what he practised in the government of his Society, he could not reprove in the government of his country.

His political philosophy had affinities with Hobbes, Locke and Rousseau. He shared the eighteenth-century view of man's blessedness in the state of nature before he entered political society. Locke had taught that reason, and Rousseau that sympathy, was the uniting bond of such a state. This latter view was the conception of Wesley who was influenced by the story of the Garden of Eden, and who drew in his *Thoughts on Slavery* an idyllic picture of Africans in a state of nature. He had no theory of the way in which people entered into a political society, but he held a theory of Sovereignty which in essence was that of Hobbes.

Both made the Sovereignty independent of the people, and endowed it with plenary authority. The only liberty Wesley claimed for the people was that 'each man without restraint could sit under his own vine.' His definition of civil liberty was 'an enjoyment of life, fortune and property in our own way.' There is no reference to any political privilege or power. Hobbes vested Sovereignty in the King, and Wesley in Parliament, but that is the only difference.

Wesley found the source of his political philosophy in the Bible. In the Old Testament, kingship was conferred by the seer as the spokesman of God. The people were not consulted, not did they share in the task of government. When a king was a good king, it was because he did what was right in the eyes of the Lord. When a king was a bad king, it was because he did that which was evil in the sight of the Lord. There was no other standard of reference. He was the vicegerent of God, not the representative of the people. It was from God that he received his authority and to God alone that he was answerable. When the Jews returned after the exile in Babylon, they set up a theocracy. This is the logical conclusion of the history of kingship in the Old Testament. It is the open acknowledgement that whoever is in authority, the real power comes only from God.

This was the view of Wesley. Rulers are given full power from God, and not from the people, and they must render account for their action to God alone. However excellent this may be in theory, it is, in practice, a dangerous doctrine to teach: but it was adopted without misgivings by Methodists after Wesley's death. Adam Clarke, in his *Origin and End of Civil Government*, not only accepted the premises and the biblical background of Wesley, but he accepted his conclusions, and gave the Sovereignty a perilously high authority. He allowed, 'the Executive may in particular cases adopt bad measures and therefore should not be vindicated in those things,' but he said, 'in general the Executive government must be supported because if not, down goes the Constitution and up rise anarchy and every possible evil.'[1] This seems to allow for possible protests against misrule, but it is counterbalanced by the general trend of his argument. 'All good subjects should avoid everything that leads to popular disaffection.'[2] In another passage he exclaimed, 'Britons, value your privileges, guard your Constitution and protect your King.... He who does anything to alienate the people's mind from loyalty to the King is worse than a public incendiary.'[3]

In his exhortation there was a very popular Methodist senti-

---

[1] J. W. Etheridge, *Life of Adam Clarke*, 1858, London, p. 311.
[2] *Origin and End of Civil Government*, by Adam Clarke, 1822, London, p. 33.
[3] *ibid.*, pp. 35, 36.

THE DOMINANT TORYISM OF METHODISM 19

ment, 'Rebellion is no cure for public evils . . . meddle not with them that are given to change.'

It was not, however, a political philosophy alone which Wesley gave to his followers; by his participation in the events of the century he gave them an example to follow. In the agitation which centres around John Wilkes, he upheld the action of Parliament in expelling Wilkes. Since the electors had the liberty of choosing a qualified person, he argued, then it was folly to speak of their being deprived of liberty because they were not allowed to choose an unqualified person. Thus he considered the arbitrary assumption of privileges by Parliament to be eminently right and proper. He did not see that the privileges of the people had been lessened, nor that the privileges of Parliament had been increased. He attacked the writer of the *Letters of Junius* because he felt the letters caused dissatisfaction with the King and his Ministers. There was no attempt in his *Free Thoughts* to discuss the conclusions of Junius. He praised the style and denounced the argument.

In the war with America, he took at first a moderate and reasonable attitude. He believed the Colonists had real grievances. He declared in a letter to Lord Dartmouth that they had a common purpose and therefore were dangerous because England was neither strong nor united.

Wesley desired in any case to avoid the horrors of war. He wrote to his preachers in America urging them to use their influence for peace. A letter to his brother Charles, written at the time, showed that he had committed himself to neither side of the dispute. He was prepared to believe there were faults on both sides, but he 'loved and prayed for both with a sincere and impartial love.'[1] Then came the outbreak of hostilities and the publication of Dr. Johnson's *Taxation no Tyranny*. Wesley was greatly influenced by both, and allowed himself to argue away his own intuition. His sense of duty demanded that his loyalty should be uncompromising. In three pamphlets, he attempted to show the colonists had no legal basis for their claims, they had already the fullest liberty they could desire, and they had shown throughout the history of the dispute, a desire for nothing less than independency.[2] His tracts had a

---

[1] March 1775.
[2] *Calm address to our American colonies. Observations on Liberty,* and *Calm address to the Inhabitants of England.*

great circulation and were widely discussed in the periodicals of the day.[1]

Wesley rendered no mean service to the Government when he forsook his early opinions, and defended the loyalist attitude to the war.

If, in the events of the century, it is possible to see the convinced Tory exercising his very considerable influence on the side of King and Constitution, it is just as easy to discern his attitude from the opinions he expressed, and even more in the things he left unsaid. He made a passing comment on the anomaly of Old Sarum having two members, Looe having four members, and every county in Wales having only one member of Parliament. On one other occasion alone, did he refer to the inadequacy of Parliamentary representation. It was once more a reference to the scandal of Old Sarum without a single inhabitant, having two members of Parliament. It is impossible on the strength of these two protests to represent Wesley as a political reformer. For him the Parliamentary system was working well, and if there were anomalies here and there, he felt it was inevitable, for no system is wholly perfect. He made one comment on the British rule in India, and lamented that it was in the hands of a company of merchants. He deplored the increase of suicides, and desired Pitt to associate ignominy and shame with it. He thought that the bodies of such people ought to hang in chains. He considered there were far too many pensions, and that many were useless and could be abolished.

He was one of the very first to plead for the abolition of distilling. He believed spirits to be deadly poison destroying the strength and morals of Englishmen. He argued that taxation was too heavy and should be reduced, and he believed that the national debt was too burdensome, and that half of it should be discharged.

Apart from these proposals, Wesley never criticized the existing institutions of the day. Parliament he praised invariably. He had no word against the Poor Law, no constructive criticisms of prisons, no condemnation of any features of the penal code. He found the Constitution as ideal as a reasonable man could expect.

It was this Wesley, a staunch Tory in action and in thought, who shaped Methodism and directed its course. It is not possible to over-estimate his influence on the political thought of Methodism

---

[1] *Gentleman's Magazine*, Vol. XLV, pp. 581–584. *Monthly Review*, 1775.

THE DOMINANT TORYISM OF METHODISM

in the Napoleonic era. The predominant conservatism which characterized the Society was derived from him. His ideas were accepted with utter fidelity. What he did intelligently, was often done blindly by others. In this way the political faith of Wesley was in danger of becoming a superstition with his followers. Such was his prestige.

This was not the sole reason, however, for the conservative attitude of Methodism. Wesley died two years after the French Revolution had begun, but he only referred to it once. Its full significance did not reach England at large until 1793. By that time the Revolution had reached its worst stage of horror. English people were revolted by stories of bloodshed and violence. It was not difficult for Pitt to introduce repressive legislation after the collapse of the mutinies of Spithead and the Nore (1797). People were so disgusted with the abuse of liberty in France that they were willing to surrender it at home. The unfortunate connexion between licence and democracy caused Methodists to be more fully persuaded that their conservatism was justified.

There was a further factor which influenced them. Democracy was associated not only with excesses but with infidelity. In France the old religion as well as the old regime had been overthrown. Men worshipped the goddess of reason. In England also, republicans were unbelievers. They looked upon organized religion as the great prop of existing institutions, and so they worked to undermine both Church and State. Tom Paine was the accepted republican leader, and he was regarded as a notorious infidel. Methodists associated democracy with irreligion, and so they remained more strongly entrenched in their Toryism. In this, they were only typical of the times. The effect of the French Revolution and the war with Napoleon was to send the Whigs into the wilderness, and temporarily to make even moderate reform impossible.

A third influence on Methodist thought was the growing wealth of the Society. Methodists profited greatly from the new industrialism, and where they did not become masters, they became foremen and managers. An influential minority found its interests increasingly bound up with the existing order of political society, and set its face against all radical reform. This minority formed a strong conservative element in Methodism. A number of writers protested against the undue influence of the rich and the constant efforts to please them.¹ George Barratt wrote: 'There has been since Wesley's day a solicitous angling for large fishes: to these anglers the taking of a salmon is of more consequence than taking an hundred sprats, and so instead of the Gospel being as at the first preached to the poor, the net has been more principally spread to enclose the rich.'² Conference as early as 1805 had in its Address spoken in similar terms: 'In some places an undue attachment to worldly business, cares and gains, with perhaps an increase of riches, prevents any growth in a heavenly and devotional spirit.' In the first years of the century those who were not pew holders had great difficulty in getting into the more popular of the London churches. A writer declared that several people of property and genteel education had become a part of the Methodist body.³ The conclusion is that Methodism was becoming more respectable, and therefore less inclined than ever to radicalism in politics.

The doctrine of scriptural holiness was another factor in shaping the conservatism of Methodist political thought. John Wesley had not only preached the need of salvation, but the possibility of perfection. This he construed in spiritual terms. 'Q. What is Christian perfection? A. The loving God with all our heart, mind, soul and strength. This implies that no wrong temper, nothing contrary to love remains in the soul, and that all our thoughts, words and actions, are governed by pure love.' In his discussion of the results of such an experience, there was only one reference to social conduct. Christian perfection must lead to exemplariness in all things. Wesley specified in particular the need to be careful in dress, in the laying out of money and in the steady seriousness of conversation.⁴ There was no detailed guidance in this for conduct in the social and economic and political relations of life.

In Wesley's own case no guidance was necessary. Even whilst he was advising his preachers not to preach politics, nor meddle in the affairs of the day, he was sending out pamphlets on every great public issue, and on all phases of the national life. He threw himself into the work of alleviating poverty, and helping the ignorant, the sick, and the distressed. He was not capable of fitting himself

---

[1] *Strictures on Methodism by a careful observer*, 1804. *Confessions of a Methodist by a Professor*, 1820.
[2] G. Barrett, *Recollections of Methodists in Lincoln*. N.D.
[3] *Strictures on Methodism by a careful observer*, 1804.
[4] 'Plain account of Christian Perfection,' *Works*, Vol. XI, p. 435.

THE DOMINANT TORYISM OF METHODISM 23

for heaven, and remaining an idle spectator of the busy world around him. In this, his practice was greater than his teaching. There was nothing in his sermons or pamphlets on Christian perfection to suggest that all life should engage the energies of the Christian.

The unfortunate consequence was that a later generation lacking Wesley's catholicity of interests, interpreted his teaching in narrow terms. Holiness very often meant personal goodness without any concern for the problems of contemporary society. Such a transcendental emphasis gave Methodist preaching an otherworldliness which was certainly not present in the age of Wesley. We do Wesley a great injustice if we imagine that his sermons dwelt largely on the pleasures of heaven. The contrary is actually the case. There are two of his sermons on the future life, extant, and neither 'The Great Assize' nor 'Of Hell' are particularly effective sermons. He said dryly in a letter to John Smith (July 10, 1747) that he was not conscious of 'profusely flinging about everlasting fire.' He preached largely on the ethical and experimental aspects of the Christian life. His sermons on sin and salvation, although they are his finest utterances, do not represent by any means the whole scope of his teaching. His sermons on the Beatitudes are a commentary on the ethical teaching of Jesus. Nor are we to conceive of his sermons as highly emotional. Wesley was a child of his age. His sermons are logical discourses, and no one was more suspicious of irrational enthusiasm and excitability. He had no patience with the ignorance which vaunted itself, nor with mere feeling divorced from right living.

> Beware of that daughter of pride, enthusiasm. Oh keep at the utmost distance from it. Give no place to a heated imagination. Do not hastily ascribe things to God. Do not easily suppose dreams, voices, impressions, visions or revelations to be from God. They may be from him. They may be from Nature. They may be from the devil..... You are in danger of enthusiasm if you despise or lightly esteem reason, knowledge or human learning; every one of which is an excellent gift from God, and may serve the noblest purposes. I advise you never to use the words wisdom, reason or knowledge by way of reproach. On the contrary pray that you may abound in them more and more.... One general inlet to enthusiasm is expecting the end without the means, expecting knowledge for instance without searching the Scriptures, and consulting the children of God; or expecting spiritual strength without constant prayer and steady watchfulness.[1]

---

[1] 'Christian Perfection,' *Works*, Vol. XI, p. 431.

This tradition of preaching was not altogether maintained after Wesley's death. Adam Clarke was a considerable scholar, and whilst Dr. Coke was not so accomplished, he was a man of culture and wide reading, and an outstanding personality. Jabez Bunting had still to make his reputation. The other men—Benson, Moore, Mather, Thompson, Bradburn, Bradford, Atmore and Entwisle—were excellent Methodist ministers but not known outside their Society. There was no one who could worthily occupy Wesley's place. The clergymen who used to assist Wesley within the limits of their parishes had become spiritual progenitors of the Evangelical Party within the Church of England. Methodism had no longer any help from clergymen. It had an increasing number of local preachers as well as the regular ministry, but on the whole their cultural level, though not as low as it had been represented, was not high. Charges against preachers both of ignorance, and fanaticism, were sufficiently common. These were often biased and therefore unreliable. It is true, however, that sermons were no longer reasoned discourses with a strongly ethical flavour. They were evangelical as became Methodists, and delivered under the constraint of strong emotion. They were other-worldly, and many dealt vividly with the future life. This was partly because at this time ethics was falling back on the intuitive criterion and feeling was replacing logic.[1] It is difficult to find many sermons which dealt with the duty of Methodists in the life of their day, apart from those of rebel ministers such as Kilham and Rayner Stephens who were expelled from the parent body. A common jibe at Methodism was its preoccupation with the world to come. Cobbett in his *Rural Rides* flings, on more than one occasion, a contemptuous sneer against Methodism. In one of his journeys he described how he passed the open window of a Methodist chapel when the service was in progress, and heard the preacher delivering with great emotion a sermon on the future life. The wicked were frightened and the godly were edified. It was a thumbnail sketch but Cobbett intended it to be typical. *The Methodist Magazine* often contained accounts of affecting death scenes.

The pulpit was of supreme importance in Methodism. If then preachers spoke of holiness in terms which divorced it from the ordinary duties of life; if they tended to look on the world and all

---

[1] A. Cobban, *Edmund Burke and the Revolt against the Eighteenth Century*, 1929, p. 234.

THE DOMINANT TORYISM OF METHODISM 25

its ways as wicked, and if they dwelt on the rewards and punishments of a future existence,[1] it was bound to make Methodists insensitive to the conditions under which they lived. Such preaching helped to keep Methodists content with things as they were. Holiness in religion so often meant *laissez-faire* in politics.

The necessity for circumspection was another reason for the conservatism of Methodists in the early nineteenth century. For a long time there was much misunderstanding about the movement. Wesley in the early days had continually to defend his Societies against the charges of Popery and disloyalty. As late as 1875 a clergyman declared that Wesley in his doctrines was a virtual Papist.[2] If, after unremitting antagonism to the Catholic Church, Methodism could be accused of sympathy with it, it is not surprising that despite fervent protestations of loyalty, Methodists were continually suspected of disaffection. In the year 1800 the Bishop of Rochester in a charge to his clergy declared that it was a dreadful aggravation of the dangers of the present crisis in the country that persons of real piety should, without knowing it, be lending aid to the common enemy, and making themselves accomplices against the Lord and His Christ. He said that English Jacobins were making a tool of Methodism just as the Illumines of Bavaria had made a tool of Freemasonry.[3] Dissenters were known to have radical views and Methodists were often confused with them. Even in 1819 there was still need of caution. John Stephens, preaching at Rotherham in that year, said that every week Leaders' Meetings were reported in revolutionary newspapers and the worst construction was put upon them.[4]

That Methodists were aware of the suspicion regarding their loyalty is obvious not only from pamphlets and sermons, but also from pastoral addresses of successive Conferences. The claim to be utterly loyal to King and Constitution and to abhor 'democratic scheming' was made so vehemently, and so often, that it must have been provoked in part by attacks and misrepresentation.

Dislike of Dissenters was a further factor which strengthened

[1] For references to this emphasis on the future life, see G. D. H. Cole, *Wm. Cobbett*, p. 275; J. Benson, *Sermons on future misery of the wicked*; Leigh Hunt, *Attempt to show the folly and danger of Methodism*; R. A. West, *Sermons of W. Dawson; Quarterly Review*, 1810.
[2] Fred Hockin, *John Wesley and Modern Wesleyanism*, 1875.
[3] *Gentleman's Magazine*, November 1800.
[4] *Proceedings of Wesley Historical Society* (1901–1902).

the conservatism of Methodist political thought. The very reasons which made Methodists prize their connexion with the Church caused them to repel any suggestion of being a dissenting body. Severance from the Church did come, but it came slowly and without deliberate intention. Wesley licensed his chapels in 1787 as Dissenting places of worship because he needed to take advantage of the Toleration Act, but he lived and died a confessed member of the Church of England. His ordination of men to the work in America in 1784, and his laying hands on Coke and, by proxy, on Asbury for the superintendence of such work, did not seem to him to have any of the implications which they possessed for others. He strove as far as he was able to keep Methodist services out of Church hours. The rule that Methodists must meet outside Church hours was not abolished till 1788. He would only allow ordained clergymen of the Church of England to administer the Sacrament, though twenty-seven men he himself ordained.[1]

His association with Dissenters was very casual. In his *Journal* there are few references. He spoke of some Dissenters being concerned in the Wednesbury riots against the Methodists.[2] In reply to a clergyman who charged him with Dissent, he protested he was a true son of the Church of England and he laid down what in his opinion constituted Dissent.[3] At another stage in his life he administered the Lord's Supper at Norwich to two hundred communicants. As a considerable part of them were Dissenters, he asked everyone to use what posture he judged best. He declared that had he required them to kneel, probably half would have sat. As it was, all but one knelt.[4]

These are his main references to Dissenters and they contrast strangely with the repeated allusions in the *Journal* to his love for the Church of England.[5] Thus the tradition of Methodism was strongly Anglican. Its early history was a record of its close association through its leaders with the Church. At no time was there such affinity with Dissenting bodies.

---

[1] Beaumont said that 'Wesley like a strong and skilful rower looked one way, while every stroke of his oar took him in an opposite direction.' (*New History of Methodism*, Vol. I, p. 488.)

[2] *Journal*, Vol. III, p. 120.

[3] *ibid.*, Vol. II, p. 338.

[4] *ibid.*, Vol. IV, p. 302.

[5] One does not forget his friendship with Philip Doddridge nor his occasional preaching in Dissenting chapels.

This separateness was still further emphasized by differences in theology and politics. The two great leaders of Dissent in the eighteenth century were Dr. Priestley and Dr. Price. Both attained national fame and had a national influence: both were confessedly radical in politics. In the War of American Independence the doughtiest opponent of Wesley was Dr. Price who wrote an extremely able book, *Observations on Civil Liberty*, in defence of the colonists. Wesley wrote his own *Observations on Liberty* expressly as an answer to it. When the French Revolution had broken out Dr. Price praised the course of events wholeheartedly from his pulpit and used his influence to secure radical reform in England. The London Revolutionary Society was largely inspired and guided by him. Many of its members were Dissenters. Joseph Priestley adopted precisely the same attitude to events. He advanced the claim of the colonies in the War of American Independence, and he supported with enthusiasm the revolution in France.

Now this radicalism in politics was allied to a radical theology. Priestley was confessedly Unitarian, and Price held substantially the same views. In 1782 Priestley's *History of the Corruptions of Christianity* was published. Wesley greatly desired Fletcher of Madeley to reply to it and in his letter said: 'I look upon everything with a jealous eye which prevents you answering Dr. Priestley. He is certainly one of the most dangerous enemies of Christianity that is now in the world. And I verily think you are the man whom God has chosen to abate his confidence.'[1]

It was unfortunate that the radical views of two leading Dissenting ministers should be associated in the public mind with all the Dissenting bodies. There was a partial justification for this but it was not an accurate representation of the attitude of Dissent. The Presbyterian and Unitarian bodies had occupied an advanced position in politics and theology. Throughout the century there was no real difference between the Unitarian and the Presbyterian conception of the person of Christ. This Arianism in religious thought had a certain influence on the Baptist and Congregational bodies, but they never adopted completely radical views either in theology or politics. It is true that a writer could speak in 1730 of the 'Decay of the Dissenting Interest,' but by the end of the eighteenth century the 360 Congregationalist chapels had become 800.

Between 1760 and 1820 12,000 chapels were registered for Non-

[1] *Letters of the Rev. John Wesley*, Vol. VII, p. 264.

conformist worship. In the nineteenth century they experienced a recrudescence of spiritual life. The pamphlets written in the first years of the century attacked the extreme radicalism of Dissent without distinguishing its separate denominations.

This widely held view of Dissent had an important effect on Methodist thought. There was in any case no love for Dissenters, and yet Methodists found themselves constantly associated with Dissenters in contemporary writings. A pamphlet which had a wide circulation classed Methodists with Dissenters and spoke of them as seditious.[1] This confusion of thought was intolerable when Dissenters were suspected of being radical in theology and politics. It caused Methodists to affirm even more strongly their orthodoxy in theology and their conservatism in politics. Many of them began to associate heresy in religion with radicalism in politics.

The conservatism of Methodism was shown in two main directions. In the first place Methodists were indifferent to abuses in the Constitution. Adam Clarke, who was so prominent a leader in the years after Wesley's death, wrote, 'The Constitution is good: it can scarcely be mended. It is the best under the sun.'[2] When Conference met in 1792, Question twenty-five asked, 'What direction shall be given concerning our conduct to the Civil Government,' and the answer was, 'None of us shall either in writing or conversation speak lightly or unworthily of the Government under which we live. We are to observe that the oracles of God command us to be subject to the higher powers, and honour to the king is connected with the fear of God.' The pastoral letter sent out by the next Conference declared the love of Methodists for their country and its Constitution, and said that Methodists would support the king and country with all they had, and all they were. This was the usual tone of Conference, and of Methodist ministers, when speaking of the Constitution and the Monarchy. Yet these were the days of the unreformed parliament; the days of public hangings at Tyburn; the days of capital punishment for trivial offences, and the days when the Poor Law operated with undue severity.

Methodism was not only indifferent to abuses, it was suspicious of reformers. This is the second feature of its conservatism. John Wesley had declared himself convinced that a republican spirit was injurious to Methodists. He said that most fallen Methodists and

[1] T. E. Owen, *Methodism Unmasked*, 1802.
[2] J. W. Etheridge, *Life of Adam Clarke*, p. 311.

perhaps some who were not fallen, were republicans.[1] This is Wesley's only reference to the effects of the French Revolution on England. The brevity and indirectness do not obscure his view of republics and republicans. This attitude was faithfully adopted by his followers. When in 1792 there were signs of disaffection in Manchester, Benson preached a sermon on obedience to the higher powers. The people, he said, had nothing to do with the laws but to obey them.[2]

Richard Carlile, who was one of the later leaders of Republicanism in England, and who suffered more than one long period of imprisonment for his views, said that the pious Methodists were circulating thousands and thousands of tracts on the drunkenness of Tom Paine.[3] It was not Republicanism, however, against which Methodism set its face, but any political reform. This attitude is perhaps understandable in the case of the Luddites. Despite the shadowy Ned Ludd, and his supposed generalship, it is difficult to discover any real co-ordination in the sporadic riots which broke out, and there seems to have been no constructive programme behind the smashing of machinery and the seizure of fire-arms. There was burning resentment against shearing frames and steam looms which appeared to be displacing man labour at a time when food was scarce and employment hard to find. One witness swore before Charles Prescott that forty-five thousand weavers had been displaced by steam looms. He said that a man with five children under eight years of age, and a wife, got twelve shillings a week and worked sometimes sixteen hours a day. He declared that many men only got eight shillings a week, and that consequently families had to live chiefly on potatoes and one pint of milk each day.[4] However dreadful their plight, it seems incredible that mere destruction should be looked upon by the Luddites as the answer to their problem. It is conceivable that some regarded the riots as a mere preliminary to a general rising. Certainly magistrates and informers when sending their reports to the Secretary of State stressed the stealing and storing of fire-arms, and asked for a strengthening of the military forces.[5] In particular, the Court House of Wakefield on

[1] *Arminian Magazine*, 1789, p. 49.
[2] Richard Treffry, *Memoirs of the Rev. Joseph Benson*, 1840.
[3] *The Republican*, Vol. VI, August 1822.
[4] Public Record Office State Papers Domestic; Home Office, 1811.
[5] Public Record Office: Luddite Riots Papers. H.O. 40. 1.

June 11, 1812, sent an urgent letter asking for a secret search for arms and the establishing of military law. This was followed by a second letter couched in similar terms on June 22. Sir Francis Wood writing to Earl Fitzwilliam declared that the riots were leading up to an insurrection.

One informer said that the Luddites spread over Nottingham, Warwick, Stafford, York, Lancaster, Chester and Derby.[1] A Luddite said in a letter that London was backward 'with only fourteen thousand twisted in.' Samuel Radcliffe, who was arrested and sentenced to transportation, said, when under sentence, 'The Union extends from London to Nottingham and thence to Manchester and Carlisle.' Allowing for exaggeration in these statements it is obvious that the disaffected in these widely different areas did not want merely to smash machinery. In the West Riding, and in districts round Stockport and Manchester, the machinery must have seemed a real menace, and here rioting was worst. In a letter to Mr. Smith of Huddersfield, 'Ned Ludd' said the Luddites were strong in Manchester, Halifax, Bradford, Sheffield, Oldham and Rochdale.[2] In other places, political discontent must have allied itself with economic grievance, and reformers must have seen in the Luddites a means to attain an end. This would account for the widespread nature of the movement and for the absence of any rigid organization or plan. There is a letter from Ned Ludd which may represent the views of some Luddites. He spoke of the strength of the Luddites and ended with a denunciation of the King and his son and the necessity for a republic.[3] T. Maitland who was in command of the forces in the disturbed districts gave as his opinion that there was no deep laid plot and that trouble was confined to the lowest.[4] Whether or no there existed any clear ideas behind the Luddite riots, none was apparent to shocked observers. The rioting seemed senseless and dangerous even to those who felt the Luddites had certain legitimate grievances. To Methodists it was simply criminal. Even the desperate poverty and the increasing unemployment of the rioters seemed not a matter for protest but for endurance. Jabez Bunting, who was to be, after Wesley, the

---

[1] Public Record Office: Luddite Riots Papers. H.O. 40. 1.
[2] P.R.O. State Papers Domestic. H.O. 40. 1.
[3] P.R.O. Ned Ludd to Mr. Smith, Holder Hill End, Huddersfield. (N.D.)
[4] P.R.O. Manchester, June 19, 1812.

THE DOMINANT TORYISM OF METHODISM 31

most powerful personality Methodism has known, became Superintendent of the Halifax Circuit in 1811. He at once opposed the Luddites most vehemently and was bitterly disliked in consequence. This hatred reached its height when he refused to bury a Luddite who had been shot near Cleckheaton. He regarded the dead man as an utter criminal and wholly unworthy of Christian burial.[1]

An equally prominent minister of that day, the Rev. Robert Newton, was stationed at Huddersfield, and he also strenuously opposed the Luddites. He took so conspicuous a part in attacking them and in preventing any spread of sympathy, that he received a letter of thanks from a magistrate for his part 'in allaying Luddite feeling and helping to preserve order.'[2]

These two men who were each to occupy the Presidential chair on four occasions, are the most famous names among a number of Methodist ministers who followed the same line of action. There seems indeed to have been among Methodists in the disturbed areas a common mind on the matter. A Methodist writer, in a book written some years after, said in a most illuminating paragraph:

> In 1812, when the infatuated populace of the West Riding of Yorkshire in the madness and wickedness of their folly visited like prowling wolves the abodes of their neighbours, exciting the most fearful apprehensions for personal safety, demolishing property and destroying life, the Methodist ministers did not shrink from the duty they owed to their country, but publicly and from house to house, laboured to counteract the influence of wicked and mischievous men. I have no wish to underrate the influence of the truly pious of other denominations, yet, my Lord, it is on record as an historical fact that Methodist ministers were, I believe, the only ministers of religion as a body who made a declaration of their sentiments at the awful crisis in an address to their Societies, in which they said, 'We look at the principles which have given birth to this state of things with the utmost horror, principles which are alike destructive to the happiness of poor and rich.'[3]

The violence, and on occasion the bloodshed which accompanied the Luddite rioting, explains, and perhaps excuses, the Methodist attitude. No such defence, however, can be made for the part

[1] G. Smith, *History of Methodism*, Vol. III, 1857.
[2] Joel Mallinson, *Methodism in Huddersfield*, 1898.
[3] 'Reasons for Methodism in a letter to the Bishop of Exeter,' 1834, p. 28.

played by Methodism in the Reform movements which were prominent between 1817 and the passing of the Reform Act in 1832.

The Conference of 1812 declared that although they were assured that the Methodist Societies were uncontaminated with the spirit of insubordination and cruelty of violence which had caused so much misery and distress, yet they could not but dread the operation of its insidious and infectious nature, and the speciousness with which it seduced simple and credulous men. They therefore sounded an alarm lest any Methodist people be drawn away by evilly disposed men and proclaimed loudly, 'Fear the Lord and the King and meddle not with them that are given to change.' The Conference said that it knew and felt for the situation of the poor. It was aware of their want of employment and the dearness of provisions, but it was convinced that murmuring and discontent would not alleviate those sufferings but would aggravate them. The Conference pleaded with the richer brethren to assist the poorer, and begged all to hope and trust in God.[1]

No words could state more plainly the attitude of official Methodism to all movements of reform. Not only in the Luddite riots but in the years following, precisely the same viewpoint was adopted. There was no recognition of the widely different nature of the later reform agitation from that of the Luddites.

The Societies for Reform which had arisen in the decade of the French Revolution were severely hit by the arrest of Horne Tooke, Hardy, and others in 1794, and following the repressive legislation of Pitt in 1797 they began rapidly to decline. Some Reformers, however, refused to lose heart. A fresh start was made in 1807, when once more, Francis Place took up the question of Parliamentary Reform. It was due to his organizing skill that Francis Burdett was returned for Westminster, and Reformers had a spokesman in Parliament. In 1811 arose the 'Society of Friends to Parliamentary Reform,' and also the Hampden Club.[2] Many other societies started on similar lines, but it was William Cobbett who more than any other gave new power to the whole movement. He had a passionate love for the English countryside and the English peasantry. He took up the cause of the people, and laid his club about him lustily in defence of their rights. He was no advocate of

---

[1] *Minutes of Conference*—Pastoral Address, 1812.
[2] See G. S. Veitch, *Genesis of Parliamentary Reform*, p. 342.

violence. For him the way of the Luddites was repugnant, and he denounced rick burning and rioting. Instead he taught people to look to the vote as the means of redress. His *Political Register* provided a forum of discussion. He became the mouthpiece of the unpropertied classes, and showed to the rich for the first time the strength of the people's case.

Through him, as much as through the new Reform societies, people began to agitate for Parliamentary reform. The Corn Law of 1815 was a further influence in stirring the people to action. It was designed to prevent the importation of cheap grain. This was a great benefit to the British wheat grower, but to no one else, for the people had to pay dearly for their bread, and were therefore deprived of much of their power to purchase other commodities. This did not please the new manufacturing classes. But if the Tories had their way in 1815, the Whigs scored a success by the abolition of the Income Tax in the next year. The triumph was illusory for it only meant heavier indirect taxation. This incidentally fell on the poor as heavily as on the rich, and they were less able to bear it. This was not apparent however to Henry Brougham, and the Whigs, who were greatly pleased with the successful outcome of their petitions and propaganda. They remained outside the agitation of the next few years. Parliamentary Reform was not as sweet-sounding as Income Tax repeal. They disliked the repressive policy of Sidmouth and the Government, but they were somewhat afraid of the radicalism of the working-class leaders. So the battle was waged by the people themselves. This agitation reached its height in 1819. There were severe restrictions on public meetings. Rioters could be imprisoned on charges of treason and printers on charges of issuing seditious literature. Periodicals were so heavily taxed that newspapers were expensive luxuries. There had been some justification for this when the French Revolution had terrified the nation, and Corresponding Societies seemed revolutionary and dangerous. In the struggle against Napoleon, the nation had borne the repressive legislation with small complaint. Now in time of peace it was unnecessary and irksome. Sidmouth, however, applied it without abatement. He even let agents and spies work freely among the Radicals. He was a narrow, hidebound Tory, and the last one capable of dealing justly with the Peterloo massacre.

There was nothing disturbing even to the Government in the crowds which gathered on St. Peter's Field, Manchester, on

August 6, 1819. From all accounts, the gathering, though very large, was orderly and quiet. The different contingents marched on to the field and took up their allotted positions. Hunt, Bamford and other leaders were most anxious to preserve discipline and order. The meeting was essentially a peaceful demonstration in favour of Parliamentary Reform. The magistrates, however, lost their heads. They allowed a troop of yeomanry to charge down on the hapless crowd. Twelve people were killed and a hundred were injured.

The affair outraged the feelings of the nation. Whigs, merchants, and of course artisans and workmen, were indignant at the cold-blooded massacre. The wrath of Radicals knew no bounds. Numbers of petitions were sent up to Parliament demanding an inquiry.[1] The answer of the Government was to thank the magistrates for the sternness they had shown. So far from setting up an inquiry, the Government proceeded in that winter to pass the 'Six Acts' whereby order was even more strictly enforced. Sidmouth had used whips, now he used scorpions.

In this outcry Methodism had no share. There is no record of a single protest against the action of the magistrates. On the contrary the Committee of Privileges 1819 expressed itself in the following terms:

> We desire to record our strong and decided disapprobation of the tumultuous assemblies which have lately been witnessed in many parts of the country, in which large masses of people have been irregularly collected. There have been wild and delusive political theories, and violent and inflammatory declamations which bring the Government into contempt. From all such public meetings the members of the Methodist Societies are asked to abstain. Ministers are asked to warn people against private political associations illegally organized: any person connected with our body persisting after due admonition in identifying himself with the factious and disloyal shall forthwith be expelled from the Society according to our established rules. The Committee have received with cordial satisfaction assurance of the loyal spirit and demeanour of our Societies in general, and devoutly trust that at this crisis, as on several similar occasions in former years, the influence of Christian principles and discipline on the poorer classes of our Society will be found highly beneficial in discountenancing the machinations of the ill-disposed, and in leading the suffering poor of our manufacturing districts, whose distress the Committee sincerely commiserate, to bear their privations with patience and to seek relief not in schemes of agitation and crime, but in

---

[1] *Parliamentary Debates* (*Hansard*), 1819.

THE DOMINANT TORYISM OF METHODISM   35

reliance on Divine Providence, and in continuous prayer for the blessing of God on our country and on themselves.[1]

This was a sweeping condemnation of the whole agitation which culminated in Peterloo. There was no attempt to discuss the merits of the Reformer's proposals, and no attempt to understand the motives which prompted the agitation. The movement seemed likely to bring the Government into contempt and therefore no Methodist could associate himself with it under pain of expulsion. This was Toryism unabashed.[2] It was in this year of Peterloo that John Stephens, a famous Methodist preacher, declared that the contest was between vile demagogues and a venerable King; between anarchy and social order.[3]

If Manchester was one centre of Parliamentary Reform propaganda, the Tyneside was a second of great importance. One of the most popular Reform societies was known as the 'Brotherhood' and its membership consisted mainly of colliers. Daniel Isaac, a Methodist minister, set himself to combat this organization, and persuaded the Methodist ministers of the Newcastle Circuit to help him. All colliers living near Methodist Societies were visited, and the evils of the Brotherhood were pointed out to them.

Those who had taken the oath were asked to abjure it, and the others not to take it. This met with some success. Many left the Brotherhood. One minor consequence was that Daniel Isaac, returning home one night, was set upon by members of the Brotherhood and severely beaten.[4] So pleased was the Duke of Northumberland with the loyalty of Methodists at this period, that he gave them fifty pounds towards a new chapel. He said it was given because Methodists discountenanced opinions which would lead to the subverting of all religion.[5]

A pamphlet printed in Newcastle at this time, accused a Methodist preacher of using his pulpit to dissuade people from going to Reform meetings. The pamphlet was a vigorous indictment of the Toryism of Methodist politics. It took the form of a dialogue

---

[1] T. P. Bunting, *Life of Jabez Bunting*, Vol. II, p. 188.
[2] The Circular had a great effect on Methodists in the disturbed areas. It confirmed them in their loyalty. Cf. 'Reasons for Methodism in a letter to the Bishop of Exeter,' 1834.
[3] *Proceedings of Wesley Historical Society* (1901–1902).
[4] G. Smith, *History of Methodism*, 1857, Vol. III, p. 517.
[5] W. W. Stamp, *The Orphan House of Wesley*, 1863, London.

between a Methodist preacher and a Reformer. The preacher was represented as bitterly opposed to Reform and as explaining to the Reformer in no ambiguous terms his final destiny. The preacher said that Methodists must always 'Seek the things that are above.'

One of the Reformer's replies throws light on the Methodist attitude to Peterloo: 'Do not run in an affected fright to a police office, as I see many Methodist preachers have done at Manchester, and join associations for the purpose of arguing with swords and batons. Your God-fearing yeomanry have sabred the people but not therefore cured them of error.'[1] Bunting brought the arm of official Methodism down on Tyneside just as at Manchester. Those suspected of radicalism were warned, and those who were unrepentant were expelled.[2]

It is a matter of historical interest that this same attitude persisted to the middle of the century. As early as 1811 there was a protest in the *Tyne Mercury* against a Methodist preacher who urged the reluctant pitmen at Jarrow to accept their bonds under pain of Hell if they refused. A long correspondence followed and 'No Methodist' asserted that some Methodists had been among the founders and supporters of the combination. Now he said, Methodist preachers were posing as its destroyers.[3] The explanation is that individual Methodists of radical views founded the combination, but official Methodism was opposed to it. A later illustration of the conservatism of official Methodism was in the suppression of the *Christian Advocate* in 1833.[4] The *Christian Advocate* was an influential Methodist paper, but because its views seemed too radical, it was banned by Conference.

The best example of the clash between individual Methodists of liberal views, and official Methodism, was the case of the Tolpuddle martyrs. They were Methodists who had joined a union for agricultural labourers in Dorset. Methodism did not attempt to help the wronged men. Their ultimate release came through the exertions of a member of Parliament and a philanthropist.[5] Methodists did not approve of trade combinations for working men.

[1] 'Dialogue between a Methodist Preacher and a Reformer,' 1819.
[2] *History of Independent Methodism in Durham and Northumberland*, R. Kelly, 1824; also T. P. Bunting, *Life of Jabez Bunting*, Vol. II, p. 168.
[3] J. L. & S. Hammond, *The Skilled Labourer, 1762-1832*.
[4] G. Smith, *History of Methodism*, Vol. III, p. 196.
[5] Joseph Dunne, M.P., and Dr. Thomas Wakley.

In the Chartist movement were some leaders of Methodist traditions and affiliations, but the Methodist Society as a whole was strongly opposed to it. It disliked the demand for secular education, the infidelity of men like O'Connor, the talk of violence, and the radicalism of the Chartist proposals. *The Watchman* was the most prominent Methodist paper in the middle years of the century, but it made no reference to Chartism. Even in 1848 the only political comments in the paper were a plea for Protestantism in politics. The *Eclectic Review* in a bitter article (August 1866) said that Wesleyans were tied down by laws which prevented them moving hands or feet, and by usages which fostered a servile spirit to the country and the legislature. The article declared that Methodists received their notions from Conference and were under the domination of a priestly hierarchy. These men, said the writer, were not likely to exert their political influence in support of any line of State Policy which might afterwards be quoted as a precedent for their entire submission.[1]

[1] Cf. H. V. Faulkner, *Chartism and the Churches*, 1916, New York.

CHAPTER II

THE UNDERLYING LIBERALISM

THE conservatism of Methodists in politics is the obvious and significant fact in the Napoleonic period and for many years later. Nevertheless it had its limits. There was an underlying liberalism due to many causes. In the first place the implications of Methodist theology were essentially liberal. It is true that the doctrine of Holiness had been given an unfortunate interpretation. In itself, however, it was a statement of belief in man's perfectibility. Salvation, the Witness of the Spirit (known as Assurance), and Sanctification are the three great doctrines of Methodism. They are all a commentary on the worth and possibilities of the individual soul. Wesley believed that man needed not a new environment but a new birth. In Methodism the note of individualism in religion is clearly sounded for the first time. Until the Reformation, Europe, under the authority of Emperor and Pope, had a certain unity, based on peoples, not yet articulate as nations, but one in their faith. England was perhaps the least touched by this sentiment of allegiance because its island position had separated it in part from the main stream of European tradition, and had hastened a national consciousness which became increasingly restive under foreign prelates, and under taxes and dues paid to Rome. When the Reformation came in England, it was because Henry VIII was able to use this nationalism to effect his own purposes. Religious considerations did play their part, but at the outset Protestantism in England was a national and political rather than a purely spiritual movement. The religious emphasis of the Reformation influenced England increasingly as the sixteenth century wore to its close. Puritanism was but Calvinism on English soil, and in the seventeenth century it gave to the Reformation a definitely religious character. In its finest flowering, Puritanism had grandeur and attractiveness, but in general its very austerity provoked a reaction. It had never captured the nation, and at the end of the century, its hold even over the minority, was diminished.

When the next century began, England as a whole had yet to

reap the full fruits of the Reformation. For Protestantism pushed to its logical conclusion was not the protest of a national Church against an international Church, but of the individual against the authority of the Church in matters of faith. It was the assertion that without need of intermediaries the individual could be saved by a personal faith in God. Calvinism with its theory of the elect and the damned could only partly sound this note. Its very exclusiveness made it intolerant.

It might be claimed that the Society of Friends were the first to work out the full implications of Protestantism, were it not that they never formulated a creed, nor prescribed a definite form of worship. Friends were democratic in the emphasis they placed on the Inner Light. George Fox declared: 'Now the Lord God opened to me by His invisible power that every man was enlightened by the Divine Light of Christ and I saw it shine through all: and they that believed it came out of condemnation and came to the Light of Life and became the children of it.' This conception of the Inner Light placed it on a higher level than reason or conscience. It was even given a higher authority than that of Scripture. Jacob Boehme was the spiritual progenitor of such teaching. He had laid stress on experience in religion and had minimized the importance of theology. In like manner George Fox relied wholly on the illumination of the soul through the operation of the Divine Spirit. This salvation he regarded as wrought directly by God upon the soul without the need of Church, Bible and Sacraments. The Inner Light, which was the seed of God, alone gave men consciousness of right and wrong, and that health of soul which was power and peace and joy. The conception was democratic because it claimed that the Inner Light is a gift of God to every man. The Quakers were staunch pioneers in the movement for abolishing slavery because they had so exalted a view of human personality. For the same reason they detested war and became uncompromising advocates of peace. Their belief in the potential capacity of every man for God, led them to strive to remove all those abuses and disabilities which hindered growth in the good life. Unhappily, the early enthusiasm abated in the eighteenth century. They ceased to propagate their views with missionary zeal, and became an exclusive society.

They wore a distinctive garb, had a distinctive mode of speech, and became absorbed in business affairs, and the cultivation of their own type of piety. In consequence, they were looked upon as a peculiar people, and they dwindled in numbers. In the nineteenth century internal division still further weakened their strength. When George Fox died in 1691 there were probably about 60,000 Friends in England, Scotland and Ireland, but there are now not more than 22,000, although their influence is out of all proportion to their numbers.

The conclusion must be, that whilst the Quakers laid emphasis on individualism in religion, it was only partially realized in practice. Their doctrine was too mystical to commend itself to the ordinary man. There was no well-defined theological creed upon which he could lay hold. There was no hymnary to carry in song the burden of the message. The meetings for worship were held with long periods of silence and without formal plan. The quietness was only broken when a member felt impelled to speak or pray. It was not possible that meetings which relied so little on external aids to worship should be popular. The Friends, finding themselves in public estimation as an exclusive sect, made no real attempt to break down that exclusiveness. Indeed they seemed to pride themselves upon it. In dress, conversation and customs they maintained their own walk of life. The consequence was, that having an essentially democratic message to proclaim, they yet failed to reach the masses of the people.

John Wesley, preaching that salvation was open to every believer, struck for perhaps the first time the full authentic note of Protestantism. Methodism was the development of the principle inherent in Protestantism, that neither State nor Church must usurp the right which belongs to the individual conscience. It asserted the place of the individual in religion.

The eighteenth century was not only the century of individualism in religion but in political thought. Rousseau was its prophet. Hobbes had defended absolutism, Locke was the apologist for limited monarchy, and now Rousseau became the spokesman of democracy. The Paris rabble in 1789 shouted his catchwords and, had they been able, would have translated his thought into action. In England, Locke was followed by Bentham, who taught the doctrine of individualism in politics. This doctrine became the accepted political philosophy of the greater part of the nineteenth century. In the second quarter of the century its influence was supreme. The close parallel between Wesley's call to individual salvation, and Bentham's call to individual energy was significant. It meant that in politics Methodists would be Benthamites distrusting the State, and relying on the unfettered individual to work out his own salvation. As in religion, they appealed to people on grounds of utility to accept the Christian faith, so in politics they were prepared to accept the same principle. It was on this same ground that Evangelicals and Benthamites were one in humanitarian reform. At first, the sole aspect of Benthamism which appealed to Methodists was the non-interference of the State with the individual. Unlike the Benthamites, however, they did not realize that if the liberty of the individual was to be extended it must be through the State. So they opposed both the Roman Catholic Relief Act of 1829 and the Combination Acts of 1824-1825. They opposed the Parliamentary Reform Act of 1832 and had no word in favour of the Municipal Reform Act of 1836. Yet the transference of power to the middle classes was a primary object and achievement of Benthamism. Thus the Benthamism of Methodists needs qualification. It was an attitude rather than a creed. It was consistent with the most reactionary Toryism, but that was not its true direction. When the implications of this philosophy of individualism were fully realized, it was bound to overstep any limits set upon it. For one cannot assert a man's worth in the eyes of God, and be content for him to remain of no account in the eyes of his fellows. To secure initiative for the individual in religion was a preliminary to claiming it for him in political life. The underlying liberalism of Methodism came largely from this emphasis on the importance of the individual soul.

This recognition of the individual is found not only in the theology of Methodism but in its Hymn Book. The Romantic Revival was not a mere 'renascence of wonder.' The 'Ancient Mariner' is truly an expression of its spirit, but so is 'The Task' and so is 'I wandered lonely as a cloud.' The Revival included the mysticism of Blake, the realism of Crabbe, the sensuousness of Wordsworth and the romanticism of Scott and Byron. It was nothing less than a revival of interest in man. It could perhaps more accurately be described as a revival of interest in men. The Renaissance had discovered the universal man just as it had discovered the solid joys of earth. There is a difference between the literature of the Middle Ages and the Renaissance, which can loosely, and somewhat inaccurately (remembering such poetry as that of Chaucer) be called the change from interest in God to interest in Man. In the literature of the Elizabethans is a love of the table, a delight in clothes and a zest for hunting and sport. There is an equal interest in the pleasures of the mind; a thirst for knowledge whether obtained from books or travel or intercourse. But one does not find a corresponding interest in the spiritual aspirations of man. This was to come with Puritanism in the seventeenth century. Nor was there any lively interest in ordinary men. Even Shakespeare, who had drawn so many characters and given them life, does not do more than sketch in a few lines any portraits from the lower classes of the community. His shepherds, artisans, soldiers, servant-men are generally drawn to type. One does not forget Bottom, Bardolph, Stephano and Trinculo, old Gobbo and many others, but in no case are they the chief characters around whom the plays revolve. Shakespeare's characters are usually people of gentle breeding. His heroes and heroines are aristocrats or of royal family. Kings and dukes are the commonplaces of his plays.

One reason for this neglect of the ordinary working man was his unimportance in the world of Society and of the State. The Renaissance was the age of absolutism: the age of Henry VIII, Francis I and Charles V. It was the time when, as Hobbes expressed it, 'a nation was unified in the unity of its representer.' The people had no share in Government. This system gave place to limited monarchy in England, when James II fled in a panic from the country, and William III accepted the Revolution settlement. Even this was government by an aristocracy. The House of Commons was almost as aristocratic as the Lords. It consisted largely of the younger sons of great houses, and of landowners and gentry. The country was ruled locally by Justices of the Peace who were also the Squires. If people had the full liberty that Wesley claimed, it was certainly not liberty to share in government. The end of the century brought the philosophy of Rousseau and the French Revolution. It was the dawn of democracy. 'Bliss was it in that dawn to be alive.' The contagion caught men's spirits and one name for the contagion is the Romantic Revival. Other influences shaped the Revival but this was fundamental. It was the emancipation of men expressed in literature. That is why there is a closer and more searching interest in men in the literature of the Romantic Revival than was possible in the Renaissance. The ordinary individual had at last come into his inheritance. In England this is marked by the philosophy of

Bentham, the literature of the Romantic Revival and the movement of John Wesley. There is no more characteristic achievement of the period than the Methodist Hymn Book. After the 'Augustan Age,' with its polished couplets reflecting the chatter of the coffee houses, and the life of town Society, the poetry of Charles Wesley was the harbinger of a new day. It broke all the canons of the classical school. It employed a variety of metres, some regular and some irregular. It expressed the theology of experience and therefore was instinct with feeling. It arose out of a missionary movement and was concerned to show the love of God for every man. It called upon 'outcasts, harlots, publicans and thieves' and assured to them the full benefits of the Christian life. Consider the emotion behind words such as these:

> My God I am thine;
> What a comfort divine,
> What a blessing to know that my Jesus is mine!
> In the heavenly lamb
> Thrice happy I am,
> And my heart it doth dance at the sound of His name.

> True pleasures abound
> In the rapturous sound;
> And whoever hath found it hath Paradise found.
> My Jesus to know,
> And feel His blood flow,
> 'Tis life everlasting, 'tis heaven below.

Perhaps the most characteristic hymn of the Methodist Revival is the hymn which appropriately is the first in the book. In it there is the same note of exultancy and the full recognition of the poorest and the vilest in the economy of God.

> O for a thousand tongues to sing
> My great Redeemer's praise,
> The glories of my God and King,
> The triumphs of His grace!

> . . . .

> He breaks the power of cancelled sin,
> He sets the prisoner free;
> His blood can make the foulest clean,
> His blood availed for me.

> He speaks, and, listening to His voice,
>   New life the dead receive,
> The mournful broken hearts rejoice,
>   The humble poor believe.
>
>   .   .   .   .
>
> See all your sins on Jesus laid:
>   The Lamb of God was slain,
> His soul was once an offering made
>   For every soul of man.

'Every soul of man' meant to Charles Wesley not the world considered as a whole, but each separate soul—

> Who did for every sinner die
> Hath surely died for me.

'Father of me and all mankind' is the first line of one of his hymns, and in another hymn he makes the antithesis even more striking—

> Thy sovereign grace to all extends,
>   Immense and unconfined;
> From age to age it never ends;
>   It reaches all mankind.
>
> Throughout the world its breadth is known,
>   Wide as infinity;
> So wide it never passed by one,
>   Or it had passed by me.

This recognition of the individual, and more especially of the hitherto unrecognized person, is a salient characteristic of the Hymn Book. The passion in seeking such people is reflected in the great hymn of Charles Wesley which begins—

> Ye neighbours and friends of Jesus draw near,

and which declares—

> The lepers from all their spots are made clean,
> The dead by His call are raised from their sin;
> In Jesu's compassion the sick find a cure,
> And gospel salvation is preached to the poor.

What the Psalms were to the Covenanters, the hymns of Charles Wesley were to the Methodists. They set the theology of John Wesley to music. They gave fresh meaning to doctrines. There can

THE UNDERLYING LIBERALISM 45

be few better ways of learning a creed than by singing it. The hymns gave to Methodists articulation, and were the vehicle of their own deepest feeling. When they sang, it was a mode of self-expression. No one would call the Hymn Book radical in tone. The hymns on public events were thanksgiving for victories, prayers in time of peril. Yet its sturdy individualism, its call to initiative and energy in the Christian calling had implications of which Charles Wesley never dreamed. It gave men a robust self-consciousness in religion: it was inevitable that sooner or later they would seek it in social and political life. To many Methodists, the one became a step to the other.

A third liberal influence on Methodist political thought, was the method of propaganda adopted. Since England became Protestant, there had been no field preaching and no itinerant preachers. The Lollards were only a memory. Religion was propagated in the parish church and in the Dissenting chapels, but John Wesley made the world his parish and so was not troubled with parish boundaries. He proclaimed the gospel in a new setting. Open-air speaking was so novel and so spectacular that great crowds collected. Sometimes the audience numbered twenty thousand. When Wesley made his last visit to Cornwall and spoke at Gwennap pit, he estimated the crowd at 'two or three and twenty thousand' his *ne plus ultra.* So the forgotten tradition of open-air speaking was revived, and with such spectacular results that the method was adopted by others. In the great Reform meetings in Lancashire and on the Tyneside, open-air gatherings were held with great success.

If the seed was sown by open-air meetings, the harvest was gathered by class meetings, in which members shared their experience and enjoyed Christian fellowship. The class meeting formed the nucleus of the local Society. This method also was adopted by political Reformers. Southey said the organization of Methodism familiarized the lower classes with the idea of combining in associations, making rules for their own government, raising funds, and communicating from one part of the kingdom to another.[1]

How closely Methodist procedure was followed on occasion, can be seen by the 'Declaration on the political Protestants of Newcastle-on-Tyne and neighbourhood.' The manifesto begins: 'Deeply lamenting the condition of our plundered and insulted country, we have resolved to unite ourselves under this denomina-

[1] Henry Jephson, *The Platform,* 1892.

tion of Political Protestants for the purposes of protesting against an infringement of our indisputable right to real representation. We do sincerely believe political ignorance has been the cause of our misery and degradation, and nothing but a firm and extensive union of the people to promote and diffuse a correct knowledge of our immutable rights, can possibly protect our country either from absolute despotism on the one hand, or a dreadful revolution on the other. We do therefore resolve to meet once a week in small classes not exceeding twenty in each class, and to subscribe a penny each for the purpose of purchasing such means of information as may be required. And we exhort all friends to radical Reform in Newcastle and neighbourhood to associate in like manner for similar purposes. Leaders of each class shall hold a meeting once a month, and to do away with suspicion we will not permit any secret transaction whatever.'[1] It is necessary to remember that Methodists met in small classes, that they paid a penny a week, and that each class had its leaders, to realize how close was the parallel.

A loyal Methodist from the North wrote to Jabez Bunting that agitators had adopted many of the distinctive features of Methodism, and he said that class meetings and district meetings were terms in common usage.[2] The method adopted by Methodists in propaganda had not only an effect on others, but the open-air and class meetings provided an excellent training ground for Methodists themselves. The system of lay preaching gave many a workmen's leader the first lesson in public speaking and control of an audience. Men found it easy to step from the pulpit on to the platform. The story of the Miners' Association in Durham and Northumberland, is, in measure, the record of local preachers, who by their probity of life, and their capacity for speaking, were able to lead the miners.[3]

The class meeting was likewise a means of expression for people who otherwise would not have had the opportunity to speak. It afforded some satisfaction for those who in the polity of the Methodist Church had otherwise no place. The servant girl could follow her mistress in telling the assembled people what God had done

[1] Political Tracts, 1819, Newcastle.
[2] T. P. Bunting, *Life of Jabez Bunting*, Vol. II, p. 166.
[3] W. M. Patterson, *Northern Primitive Methodism*, 1909. John Wilson, *Memoirs of a Labour Leader*, 1910. E. Welbourne, *The Miners' Unions of Northumberland and Durham*, 1923.

for her. The leader of the class might be the manager of the local factory or he might be one of the workmen engaged there. On the class-leaders' book, as members to be visited, could be found people with every variety of occupation. The social grades were brought to a common level, when each week, people met together to pray, and praise, and share their experience. The democracy of the class meeting helped to undermine the Toryism of official Methodism.

Perhaps the main reason for the liberalism which was incipient in Methodism lay in none of these things. The change from Toryism to the comparative liberalism of Methodism was due to the economic and social status of the Methodist Society. Toryism was strongly attached to the land and the Church. Liberalism drew its strength as the century wore on from the new industrial classes and from Nonconformity. Now Methodists were drawn from the industrial areas, and as the old ties with the Church were loosened they drew closer to Dissenters. The time came when the former close connexion with the Church was forgotten and Methodists regarded themselves as Nonconformists. A Church that drew its members from the new industrial middle classes, and had become allied with Nonconformity, could not remain Tory in politics. As the years passed the change to more radical views was bound to come.

This liberalism, fostered by the theology and the Hymn Book of Methodism, and by its propaganda and its social status, was manifested in two ways. It lead to secessions from Methodism by men who desired more democratic government, and it produced individual leaders in Methodism who flouted the opinion of the Church and became leaders of Reform agitation.

It is difficult to realize how bitter was the feeling against the despotic government of Methodism in the nineteenth century. There was more than one pamphlet in Wesley's own lifetime protesting against his autocracy, and his refusal to allow any laymen a share in government. But reverence for his authority and his character stifled direct criticism. Wesley said: 'The greater the share the people have in government the less liberty civil or religious does a nation enjoy. Accordingly there is most liberty in a limited monarchy, less under an aristocracy and least under a democracy.'[1] He was therefore logical in keeping people from any share in govern-

[1] *Some Observations on Liberty*, 1776.

ment; in this practice he was followed by his preachers. The result was that pamphlets began to appear condemning the despotism of Conference. Many of these came from Alexander Kilham and those who sympathized with him in his protest.

Others came from disgruntled laymen who desired drastic Reform.[1] A strong attack came from a former trustee of the Wesleyan Society who said that in Conference there was, (1) a fixed distrust of the people, (2) a degrading estimation of their own ability, (3) a determination to continue their own paymaster, (4) to make laws for themselves and the people, (5) to maintain the exclusive powers inviolate, (6) to transmit the system.[2] Another pamphlet was called, significantly, 'A free inquiry into mutual deliberation and liberty of conscience as the only bonds of lasting union, exemplified from the sentiments of preachers and friends published in near fifty pamphlets and letters 1796.' This pamphlet was signed by many laymen in the Newcastle and Sunderland districts and their aims were, (1) that each Circuit should form a committee of correspondence, (2) that delegates be sent from each Circuit to wait on the preachers at the ensuing District Meeting with an address from the first quarter day, (3) that delegates be sent from each District to attend Conference on this business.

Another letter was addressed to Messrs. Pawson and Mather, two prominent ministers, from thirteen preachers of the Nottingham District Meeting, urging that money accounts be made public. This is an indication that not only laymen, but preachers, were mildly affected by the radicalism of the early revolutionary period. It is not mere coincidence that three of the great Reform agitations which disturbed and divided Methodism arose just after the three revolutionary years of 1789, 1830 and 1848. The leaders of the movements were radical in politics and in the congenial atmosphere of those years they urged their democratic Reforms. In Kilham's case, he and his friends were freely accused of being Republicans. Mather, Pawson and Benson spoke of 'his levelling principles' and accused him and his followers of being disciples of Tom Paine.[3] His politics were revolutionary indeed compared with those of Benson, but his plea for democratic reform in the Society was studiously moderate. At his trial he protested against the power of

[1] Wesleyan Tracts, 22 Pamphlets 1792–1807. (British Museum.)
[2] *Apology for M.N.C.*, by a Trustee and a Layman, 1815. Hanley.
[3] *Defence of Alexander Kilham at his Trial*, 1796.

the preachers,[1] but his expulsion followed his failure to sign the Plan of Pacification, 1795. This Plan gave to local Societies the right to arrange services at times most suitable to them, and ministers were allowed to administer the Sacrament. It meant in effect a final separation from the Church of England. Kilham refused to sign, not because the Plan went too far, but because it was not sufficiently drastic. He felt that to secure the rights of the laity, it was necessary to introduce more thorough reforms. The Plan still preserved the ultimate authority of the Conference of preachers, and gave it the right to withdraw the privileges it had granted. Kilham published his reasons for not signing the Plan of Pacification in a pamphlet entitled 'The Progress of Liberty amongst the People called Methodists. To which is added the outline of a Constitution. Humbly recommended to the serious consideration of the preachers and people late in Connexion with Mr. Wesley.' The publication of the pamphlet led to his trial at the Newcastle District Meeting and his expulsion from Conference, 1796.

Kilham pleaded in his writings for the consent of members before any one was admitted or expelled from the local Society. He asked that local preachers should be examined before the Leaders' meeting and the Circuit meeting. He said that those entering the regular ministry should first of all be approved by the Circuit meeting; that lay delegates should be appointed by the Circuit meeting to the District Meeting, and by the District Meeting to the Conference of preachers. It was his belief that laymen and preachers ought to act together for the spiritual and temporal welfare of the whole Society.[2]

The irony is that many of the proposals for which Kilham was expelled were adopted later, and became part of the polity of Wesleyan Methodism. There is now an examination of local preachers, a Representative Session at both Synods and Conference, consisting of preachers and laymen. The laity are also represented on Connexional Committees. In the year following Kilham's expulsion, Conference conceded part of his claims. Leaders of local Societies were given the right of veto on the admission and expulsion of members and on the officers of the Society. Conference still retained, however, the right of a preacher to make all nominations.

[1] *ibid.* Also T. Shaw, 'Letter to Mr. Benson,' 1797.
[2] *New History of Methodism*, Vol. I, p. 492.

No meeting could be lawful without him being present. Laymen were not eligible for District Meetings, and Conference refused to recognize the members of the Methodist Church as the real source of authority. This was intolerable to those who shared Kilham's views. Three preachers (William Thom, Stephen Eversfield and Alexander Cummin) met Kilham, and in the Ebenezer Chapel, Leeds, the Methodist New Connexion was formed. The Connexion had a desperate struggle to survive in its early days. Members, and especially preachers, were called Jacobins, Paineites, Levellers, and Revolutionaries.[1] It emerged from its difficulties successfully and in 1814 there were 8,292 members, 207 churches, 44 ministers and 229 local preachers, in the Society.

Kilham had kindled an agitation which did not cease with his expulsion. His own devotion and enthusiasm in evangelical enterprise aroused respect and a greater willingness to understand his case. His opinions, bravely maintained in the face of bitter opposition, only increased the admiration many had for him. There was wide dissatisfaction with the conduct of Conference following his trial and expulsion. He had been indicted on making false charges against preachers, and about the money accounts, and his pamphlets had been condemned as slanderous. Such charges everybody knew to be subsidiary, and taken alone, could be attributed to his receiving wrong information, and to his over-zealous temperament. The real issues had been avoided by the Conference. The main charges against him ought to have been his plea for democratic Church government, and his plea for a complete separation from the Church of England. These two great principles for which he stood were tacitly ignored. The silence of Conference could not be communicated to the Methodist body. Many who felt the decision of Conference to be right, felt that the means by which its decision had been reached were wrong. The cause of Kilham was further helped by his ready pen. He was able to write easily and well and to attack with point and pungency. He had the added advantage of believing passionately in what he wrote. His views he did not regard as opinions, but as convictions, for which he was willing to sacrifice all. His revelation of the attitude of prominent ministers caused many Methodists pain, if not surprise. He quoted Coke as saying that 'We have the most perfect aristocracy existing perhaps on God's earth. The people have no power; we have the whole in the

[1] *New History of Methodism*, Vol. I, p. 502.

fullest sense which can be conceived.'[1] This laying bare, not of his own mind only, but that of his opponents, made a great impression on Methodism. Circulars were printed, urging a consideration of the changes he had proposed. Manchester, Huddersfield, Sheffield and Stockport sent delegates to the Conference of 1797 with the express command to insist on the admission of lay members to Conference and the District Meetings. Petitions were received by Conference in which the rights of the laity to government were urged. The result was, as we have seen, that Conference made certain small concessions. These did not satisfy the delegates to Conference, and they pleaded that the preachers should admit two or more delegates to sit with them in Conference, and assist both in the administration of finance, and the conduct of the Societies. Unsuccessful in this petition, the delegates asked that a certain number of laymen, chosen by Quarterly Meetings, should together with the preachers form the District Meetings. From these meetings, an equal number of the preachers and laity would be appointed to Conference. This was refused at once. The point was not to be gained until 1877, and even then the laity were outnumbered in the representative session of Conference by two to one. The significant thing is not the rejection of the proposals but that such proposals should ever have been made. It indicates that a radical sentiment was present in the earliest days of Methodist history.

The rise of Bible Christian Methodists was due to different causes. William O'Bryan had shown remarkable gifts as a preacher and organizer before he applied to a Wesleyan District Meeting, 1810, to be accepted as an Itinerant. His age and the fact that he was married and had a family, caused the meeting to reject his candidature. O'Bryan came of wealthy parents, and guaranteed to support his family, but he could not prevail upon the meeting. This rebuff did not quench his zeal. He continued to preach and evangelize new areas. In Devon, where Wesleyan Methodism was very weak, he had great success. As Wesley had refused to be checked by parish boundaries, so O'Bryan refused to be daunted by Circuit boundaries. He went wherever he was needed and this incurred the anger of Circuit Superintendents. In the same year that his candidature was rejected, he himself was expelled from the Methodist Society for his irregularities in preaching. Nevertheless,

[1] 'Cardinal Examination of the London Methodist Bill.'

he continued to preach and to establish new Societies, concentrating on those parishes in Devon where there was no Methodist chapel. In 1814, thanks to the wise understanding and sympathetic friendship of James Odgers, Superintendent of the Bodmin Circuit, he was persuaded to rejoin the Methodists and to add his newly-founded Societies to those of Methodism. Unhappily other preachers were not as wise as Odgers. He was given the opportunity of working in the Stratton Wesleyan Mission, but the superintendent minister would not preach where O'Bryan preached. His own chapel expelled him from membership because he was absent from the class meeting on his missionary labours for three weeks in succession. The Church of England had not been sufficiently elastic to absorb the Methodist Society, and now Methodism itself was too rigid an organization to find room for a free lance such as William O'Bryan.

When O'Bryan separated himself from the Wesleyan Methodists it was not a secession as that of Kilham had been. Very few of the members he had brought into the Wesleyan Society left with him. He continued to labour in North Devon in order to reach those who were unattached to Methodist chapels. He was invited to Shebbear and after some hesitation he enrolled twenty-two people in a class. For a time these people went to church and had their own services at a later hour. But a new vicar was appointed, and according to James Thorne (one of O'Bryan's chief associates), there was no Christ in his gospel. It was decided to build a chapel and so began the Bible Christians, 1815.

It was not until 1819 that the first Conference was held and by that time there were 2,389 members and 12 itinerant preachers. The strength of the Connexion, then as always, was in the West Country.

Although the Bible Christians seemed to have risen because O'Bryan could not be accommodated in the Wesleyan body, there were far deeper causes. It is significant that the polity of the Bible Christians was very similar to that of the Methodist New Connexion. Laymen were represented both in the District Meeting and at Conference. The Bible Christians had one unusual feature of Government. At every fifth Conference the ministers and laity were equally represented to prevent Conference from becoming a domination by priests. People complained that O'Bryan 'travelled as a preacher on the plan of the Kilhamites.'[1]

[1] *New History of Methodism*, Vol. I, p. 513.

THE UNDERLYING LIBERALISM 53

In each Connexion the rights of the laity in government were conceded. The Bible Christians might easily have been absorbed into the Methodist New Connexion during the early years, were it not that the strength of the Methodist New Connexion lay in the North, and Bible Christians were confined to Devon and Cornwall.

When communications had become more rapid, and the North and West of England were drawn more closely together, the two Connexions had developed along their own lines and created their own traditions. It was too late to think of absorption. They continued their separate existence until 1907, when they united with the United Methodist Free Churches to form a single body known as the United Methodist Church. Alexander Kilham and William O'Bryan are not to be regarded as lonely agitators. They spoke for many others when, in fidelity to their principles, they left Wesleyan Methodism, and set up Societies conceived on more liberal lines.

That the Toryism of the Methodist Society was not always that of individual members is shown by other secessions which occurred throughout the first half of the century. Such secessions were always in part a protest against the despotism of Conference. They led to the formation of smaller Methodist bodies which had a more democratic system of government and which gave greater scope to the laity.

It is a sad commentary on the history of religious revivals that within twenty-five years of Wesley's death Hugh Bourne was thrust out of the parent Society for his irregular methods in evangelism. In so short a time the organization of Methodism had become rigid. The established Church could find no place for men who ignored parish boundaries. The Wesleyan Society could find no place for men who ignored Circuit boundaries. The meetings on Mow Cop seemed as dangerous and irregular a proceeding to the ministers of Burslem and district as Wesley's open-air preaching had seemed to the clergy of his day. In each case it was tacitly felt that the regular machinery of the Church was sufficient to reach the people and that mass meetings of the people were to be deprecated. From the standpoint of caution and good sense, they were doubtless justified. In the case of camp meetings, especially, there was a real danger that the remoteness of the place, and the wild enthusiasm engendered, might lead to disorderly behaviour and actual immorality.

Hugh Bourne felt that any such risks were justified by the evident tokens of God's blessing on the method adopted. The revival at Harriseahead in 1802 had been followed by a second one in 1804, and the effects of the revival were still manifest in 1806. It was at this time that Hugh Bourne, wholly zealous for evangelistic enterprise, met Lorenzo Dow. Dow had come from America, where camp meetings had been held which lasted two or three days, and which attracted thousands of people. He kindled Bourne's imagination and it seemed that such meetings might be transplanted to English soil. The first camp meeting was held on May 31, 1807. People came in great numbers to learn what camp meetings were like. Some had come from Yorkshire, and some had even come from Ireland. The original plan of one platform had to be abandoned, and four preaching stands were formed out of the stones on the bare hillside. The success was so startling that it was decided to hold another. This provoked the preachers of the Burslem and Macclesfield Circuits. They printed circulars denouncing camp meetings, but despite this opposition, the second Mow Cop meeting (July 19) was as fruitful in results as the first. When the Conference met at Liverpool some days later, the camp meetings were condemned as 'highly improper and likely to be of considerable mischief.' Despite this ban, a third camp meeting was held at Norton-on-the-Moors on August 23. It was after this meeting that Hugh Bourne was expelled by the Burslem Circuit Quarterly meeting in June 1808. As with O'Bryan, the nominal charge was failure to attend his class meeting. The Superintendent told him afterwards that the real reason was that 'he had a tendency to set up other than the ordinary worship.' Even now the followers of Bourne acted as auxiliaries to the regular societies. The Societies formed by him were given loose protection by the older body, but in March 1810 the Burslem Circuit refused to take over the Society at Stanley. This widened the breach between regular and camp-meeting Methodists. Many regard the date as the birth of Primitive Methodism. Actually there were other events of equal importance. In September 1810 the Burslem Society expelled William Clowes for attending the camp meetings. Many followed of their own accord out of sympathy for the man and his views. They met for worship in a house at Tunstall and for two years a weekly service was held. 'The Kitchen Church' was regarded with great displeasure by official Methodism in Burslem, and James Steele was deprived of his Sunday-school superintendency, and his leadership of two classes, because he attended a love feast there. Clowes and Steele had many followers, and soon the house became the centre of a small Circuit. In 1811 common cause was made with the camp-meeting Methodists, and on May 30 it was agreed to issue Society tickets. At successive meetings William Clowes, and a certain Crawfoot, were set apart for the work of Evangelism (July 26, 1811), and the name Primitive Methodist was adopted (February 13, 1812).

The interesting feature of this secession is that the leaders felt fettered in their desire to do the work of Evangelists. They desired by every means to reach some. Thwarted in their purpose by the rigid organization of the mother Church, they were obliged by pressure of circumstances to form a sect of their own. It lies outside the scope of this book to show how they nearly fell into the pit from which they had climbed. They consolidated their work in the Tunstall Circuit, and were only saved from eventual extinction by the resource and aggressiveness of Hugh Bourne. It was his policy of extension rather than over-carefulness about consolidation which led to the great development of Primitive Methodism in the next twenty-five years.

Although the direct cause of the separation was the desire for greater freedom in evangelism, there were other subsidiary causes. Regarded from one aspect, the assertion of the right to evangelize was a protest of the laity against the authority of the regular ministry. It was the declaration that men were not to be circumscribed in action by a literal interpretation of Methodist polity. How truly democratic was the movement may be realized by the rules of Conference drawn up in 1814. The laity outnumbered the regular ministry by two representatives to one. This rule applied both to the District Meetings and to the Conference. The ministry of women was encouraged and among the itinerant preachers some women found a place. It has been estimated that in 1832 thirteen women were appointed to preaching stations.[1] Many more women served as local preachers. From the start Primitive Methodism had an honourable reputation for its democratic views and for its advocacy of the cause of the people.

But it is not in the secessions alone, that Liberalism was shown. There were many Methodists of radical views who became leaders

[1] *Minutes of Conference*, 1832. (See *New History of Methodism*, Vol. I, p. 585.)

of Reform. This of course is noticeably evident in the Chartist movement. J. Rayner Stephens was actually a Wesleyan minister, whose radicalism was not confined to the platform, but who used his pulpit freely for his views on social and political reform. The Conference asked him to withdraw from party politics; he refused and left the ministry in 1834. He became one of the greatest Chartist leaders, and his eloquence always attracted great crowds of people. His plea for better social conditions and for political reform had a strong religious basis. His influence over the movement was wholesome, but he disapproved of the later developments of Chartism and ceased to take an active part. In the early days, however, few men were more important.[1] Thomas Cooper was another prominent leader of the Chartists who was reared in Methodism. He left because of the harsh autocratic behaviour of two superintendent ministers. In his fascinating and informative book[2] he mentions men such as Joseph Markham who were local preachers and yet Chartist leaders in their community.[3]

The history of Primitive Methodism especially in the northern counties is from one aspect a record of working-class agitation. The report of the Royal Commissioners on the Mining Districts in 1846 declared that in the great Miners' Strike of 1844 frequent meetings were held in chapels, generally those of the Primitive Methodists, and that prayers were publicly offered for the successful result of the strike and that faith might be strengthened.[4] A remarkable tribute is paid by Sidney Webb to Methodism in Durham:

> Into a community ignored by statesmen, and given up as hopeless by cleric and philanthropist, came the two inspiring influences between 1821 and 1850 of religion and trade unionism. 'The Ranters'[5] did great work from village to village. Families were transformed, and these men stood out as men of character gaining the respect of their fellows. . . . From the very beginning of the Trade Union movement among the miners, of the Co-operative movement among all sections of wage earners, of the formation of Friendly Societies, and of the attempts at adult education, it is the men who are Methodists in Durham County, especially Primitive Methodists, who take the lead and fill posts of influence. From their ranks have come an astonishingly large proportion of Trade Union leaders, from

---

[1] Frank Rosenblatt, *The Chartist Movement*, also H. V. Faulkner, *Chartism and the Churches*, 1916.
[2] *Life of Thomas Cooper by himself*, 1897.
[3] Both Lovett and Barker were former Methodists.
[4] C. R. Fay, *Life and Labour in the Nineteenth Century*, p. 187.
[5] Primitive Methodists.

THE UNDERLYING LIBERALISM 57

checkweighers and lodge chairman to county officials. They furnish to-day in the county most of the Justices of the Peace and members of Commons. ... It still remains true that in solid silent membership of every popular movement in the county from Trade Unionism, and from Friendly and Temperance Societies, right up to the Labour Party itself, no less than among their active local organizers and leaders, perhaps the largest part is contributed by the various branches of the Methodist community. ... Trade unionism was itself largely a result of the elevation of character brought by religious conversion on individual leaders.[1]

This is a notable tribute. It is borne out by the patient investigations of those who have written the history of the county. The Ranters denounced drunkenness and gambling. They made the chapels centres of communal life and activity. They gave the pitmen Bible authority for their demands. In the earliest assemblies the pitmen came in the various lodges to the meetings with Bible texts on their banners. When Co-operative Stores were opened in the villages, it was usually Methodists who were chosen as managers, because of their integrity. The biographies of such men as John Wilson, and Thomas Burt, show how much the influence of Methodism counted in shaping the outlook, and developing the gifts, of certain working-class leaders.[2]

Whilst it is easy to trace the radicalism of individual Methodists in the growth of Miners' Unions in Durham and Northumberland and in the Chartist movement, there were radicals in Methodism from the time of Wesley's death. At that time an Exeter Methodist preacher, Winterbottom by name, had been indicted for calling the reduction of the debt 'taking money out of one pocket and putting it in the other.'[3] Samuel Bradburn, who was the great orator of Methodism and one of its earlier Presidents, was freely accused of Jacobinism. It must have been interesting to sit in City Road Chapel in those days and hear Bradburn the Radical speak on one

---

[1] Sidney Webb, *Story of the Durham Miner*, 1921, extracts from pp. 21, 23, 24, 25. See especially E. Welbourne (*The Miners' Union of Northumberland and Durham*), 1923. John Wilson, *History of Durham Miners' Association*, 1907. Rd. Fynes, *Miners of Northumberland and Durham*, Blyth, 1873. G. W. Parkinson, *True Stories of Durham Pit Life*, 1912. James Everett, *The Allens of Shiney Row*, 1868.

[2] John Wilson *Memoirs of a Labour Leader*, 1907. Thomas Burt, *An Autobiography*, 1924.

[3] State Trials XXII. 825. Quoted by Birley, *English Jacobins*, 1789–1802.

Sunday and Benson the Tory on the next Sunday.¹ Adam Clarke declared that Samuel Bradburn taught the 'lowest republicanism.'² John Stephens, not to be confused with his radical son, preached a sermon in 1810 at Rotherham, in which he said that a few Methodist preachers had yielded to Jacobinism, when that fever was at its height, but he said their sins found them out, and they had been driven from a Connexion to which they were a disgrace. The point of interest is not the Toryism of Stephens but the radicalism of at least some of his brethren. One of the very first Radical Clubs to be formed at the close of the Napoleonic era was the Oldham Union Society. The first President was William Browe, and Browe was not only a journeyman machine maker but a Methodist local preacher.³

Henry Anderton, another prominent radical, was a Methodist local preacher. He gave great help to Henry Hunt when Hunt stood for Parliament in 1830. Anderton announced himself as the 'friend of universal freedom and the civil emancipation of the working classes,' and he said that he would give every man of sound mind and good morals a vote, and that he would protect that vote by ballot.⁴ Another friend of Hunt was Samuel Bamford, who stood with him on the platform at Peterloo, and who appealed unsuccessfully to present the case of the Reformers after the Peterloo massacre at the Bar of the House of Commons.⁵ Bamford had Methodist affiliations.⁶ A prime mover in the Federation of the Societies of Frame Work Knitters 1813, was Latham. Latham was a Methodist.

Jeremiah Betrell complained to Bunting that 'we have had considerable trial from those who were degenerated by Jacobinism and by zeal for a new system of religious government, and we have felt the unpleasant effects of their opinions in many places.'⁷ It was the voice of a zealous Tory offended by radicalism at close quarters.

In the great Radical Reform meeting held on the Town Moor, Newcastle, in 1819, one of the speakers was a local preacher of North Shields. A certain Mr. Wawn, who was horrified, said that the preachers were divided in their opinion. He hoped that no considerable proportion of the brethren were among them, but he

¹ Abel Stevens, *History of Methodism*, Vol. III, p. 8.
² *ibid*.
³ H. W. C. Davis, *The Age of Grey and Peel*, p. 177, 1929.
⁴ W. Pilkington, *Makers of Early Methodism in Preston*, p. 182, 1890.
⁵ Parliamentary Debates (*Hansard*), November 30, 1819.
⁶ J. L. Hammond, *The Skilled Labourer, 1760–1832*, p. 230.
⁷ T. P. Bunting, *Life of Jabez Bunting*, Vol. I, p. 132.

THE UNDERLYING LIBERALISM

knew that a small number were most determined friends to the Reformers, and he said in disgust that some of the misguided sisterhood had helped to mark their colours.[1] We know from another source, what happened to the North Shields local preacher. He was tried at North Shields by his fellow local preachers, and after a heated discussion he was acquitted. It was said, however, that he taught politics, and on this charge he was expelled by the action of the regular ministry.[2] Two other preachers of the Gateshead Circuit were present at the Reform meeting but took no part in the proceedings. They were threatened with expulsion unless they refrained from politics. This undertaking they refused to give, and with twenty other people they withdrew.[3] So began the Independent Methodist Church in the North. In consequence of the Reform meetings in 1819 at Manchester and Newcastle, Conference in that year decided to expel any person who persisted after due warning in identifying himself with 'the factious and disloyal.'

The conclusion is, I think, that there were individual radicals among the laymen, and to a much less degree among the preachers, after Wesley's death. It was not so obvious during the Napoleonic War, but afterwards in the agitation for Reform, and later, in the Chartist movement, it became increasingly evident.

At the end of the nineteenth century Methodism had still a strong conservative element but there was an even stronger element of liberalism. In the generation after Wesley, however, there was no indication of this transformation of thought. The dominant political faith was Toryism. The dislike of Radicalism does not necessarily imply Toryism. There were many moderate Whigs who looked on extreme Radicalism with disfavour, and some Methodists would doubtless call themselves Whigs in politics. But the Society as a whole was fierce in its denunciation of all attempts at political reform. It was unalterably opposed to Roman Catholic relief. It was fervid in its love of King and Constitution. It was more closely allied with the Church than with Dissenters. Finally, it strongly approved the reactionary Tory government of the day. This meant that the political faith of the Society was not Whig but Tory. People of more liberal views though present were few in number. Their day was yet to come.

[1] *ibid.*, Vol. II, p. 188.
[2] H. Kelly, *Impartial History of Independent Methodism in Durham and Northumberland*, 1824, Newcastle.   [3] *ibid.*

PART II

METHODISM AND THE EVENTS OF THE PERIOD

CHAPTER I

THE AGITATION AGAINST SLAVERY

THE traffic in slaves between Africa and America was allowed to go unchecked for two centuries without disturbing men's peace of mind. The *British Critic* recorded with surprise that not until Bishop Warburton had inveighed against the traffic in 1766 had a single suspicion arisen concerning its unlawfulness.[1]

This was not strictly accurate. As early as 1671 George Fox declared for emancipation of the slaves, and throughout the eighteenth century the Quakers stoutly opposed the traffic. In 1727, by formal resolution the Society of Friends condemned slavery and the ownership of slaves. In 1761 all Friends connected with the traffic were expelled. In Pennsylvania by resolutions passed in 1774 and 1776 no Friends were allowed to be slave holders.[2]

Other voices were raised. Godwin, an Anglican clergyman, and Richard Baxter had made early protests. The philosophy of Shaftesbury, Locke, Montesquieu and later Rousseau, encouraged belief in the natural goodness of man and made possible the conception of the simple and noble savage. Travel books such as those of Pinkerton, John Cooke, Dampier, Anson and James Cooke had spoken of the savages as noble and simple in their lives.[3]

Amongst the poets, James Thomson had in his poem 'The Seasons' (1726-1730) depicted the horrors of slavery. He was followed later by Burns who preached the essential equality of men—'A Man's a man for a' that'; Blake, whose humanitarianism was outraged by indignity to man or beast; Cowper, who strenuously opposed the traffic in slaves, and Crabbe, who consistently pleaded the cause of the common man concerned with the common things of life.

In general literature, Daniel Defoe had drawn a sympathetic study of a negro in Crusoe's Man Friday. A negro was the hero of Mrs. Aphra Benn's novel, *Oroonoko*. It was an unknown Quaker whose writings had the most considerable influence in this earlier

[1] *British Critic*, 1794, p. 181.
[2] F. J. Klingberg, *The Anti-slavery Movement in England*.
[3] *ibid*.

period of slave agitation. Anthony Benezet published in 1762 his *Account of that part of Africa inhabited by Negroes*. Five years later he published his *Caution to Great Britain on the state of the Negroes*. Then in 1767 he wrote his *Account of Guinea*, a book which affected Clarkson so greatly. It was through the works of Benezet that Wesley himself came to take an active interest in the slave trade.

Thus the *British Critic* was not wholly right in placing the beginnings of agitation against the slave trade in the middle of the eighteenth century. It was right, however, in its main contention. There had been a thin trickle of writers and speakers who opposed slavery, but the mass of people accepted the rightness of slavery without question. The *Political State* throughout all its numbers between 1720 and 1740 never once condemned it. The nearest approach was to print a letter indicating the cruelty of some slave owners.

No bishop, apart from Dr. Warburton, made a stand against it. Even George Whitefield, known on two continents as a great evangelist, kept fifty slaves in his Orphan House at Georgia, and could not reach a definite conclusion on the ethics of slavery.[1] The utmost he could do was to express great indignation with those slave owners who treated their dogs better than their slaves and made horses work less than their human cattle.[2] But Whitefield was not regarded with any less admiration because he was an owner of slaves.

If religious leaders had not committed themselves, it will be seen that Wesley was still a pioneer when he attacked slavery in his able pamphlet, *Thoughts on Slavery*, published in 1774. He accepted the eighteenth-century estimate of negroes as simple innocent creatures living a happy carefree life in idyllic conditions. This picture enabled him to draw a startling and effective contrast between that and their life in slavery. He described in detail the brutal manner of their capture, the unspeakable horrors of the outward passage, and lastly the fiendishly cruel treatment meted out to them by their owners.

In his second section he refuted the three grounds on which slavery was held to be justified.[3] In answer to anyone who might

[1] 'To Maryland' in the *Political State*, p. 21, July 1740.
[2] William Stevens, *The Slave in History*, p. 154.
[3] i.e., If a man is captured in war: if a man sells himself: if a man is the son of slaves.

say that whether just or not it was necessary, Wesley proceeded to show there was no necessity for it. The closing pages of his pamphlet were a passionate appeal to captains, merchants and planters. He bade them do away with 'all whips, all chains and all compulsion.' The captain ought to quit the traffic; the merchant ought to obey his conscience; the planter ought to spill no more innocent blood.

The picture was overdrawn. Wesley was misled in his ideas of the African's home life. He was equally credulous in accepting stories of their later existence as slaves. Not every slave owner was as cruel as Wesley would have us believe. But the book served its purpose. The inaccuracies which would have marred it as a textbook, actually helped its sale. For the whole effect was to heighten the contrast between the former happiness of the slave and his present misery. The book was well received by the Press. The *Monthly Review* actually praised the exactness of the facts collected as well as the lucid style.[1] It was to this paper that Wesley wrote a letter describing the manner in which slave holders treated their runaway slaves.[2] A direct outcome of Wesley's writings was the decision taken by the American Methodist Conference, 1790, to regard every person holding slaves, as acting contrary to the laws of God and Man.

If there is any weakness in Wesley's writing, it is that he did not envisage any State action to abolish the slave trade. He saw no hope beyond a personal appeal to the people directly concerned. So he addressed himself not to the Government, but to captains, merchants, and planters. This was, of course, in accord with his belief in self-initiative rather than State help.

It is necessary, however, to remember that he inspired and helped those who led the crusade against the slave trade.

He encouraged the Committee for the Abolition of the Slave Trade, formed in 1787, by two letters in which he stated the strength of the vested interests opposed to them and advised them on the procuring of evidence. His strong convictions on the subject of evidence collected was further shown by his letter to Granville Sharpe (October 11, 1787), in which he expressed his disapproval of the method for collecting evidence. Wesley had no patience for the hired informer.

[1] *Monthly Review*, Vol. III, p. 234, 1774.
[2] *ibid.*, p. 487.

Wilberforce was not an intimate friend of John Wesley. It was difficult to form a friendship with one who had no settled habitation. Doctor Johnson had complained that when he wanted to cross his legs and talk at leisure it was time for the rogue to go. Wilberforce found it easier to cultivate the friendship of Charles, who had a more settled existence in London. He has left on record the impression that Charles Wesley with his white hair and venerable appearance made on him: 'When I came into the room Charles Wesley rose from the table around which a numerous party sat at tea, and coming forward to me gave me solemnly his blessing. I was scarcely ever more affected. Such was the effect of his manner and appearance that it altogether upset me, and I burst into tears unable to restrain myself.'[1] So great was the respect of Wilberforce that when Charles Wesley died he arranged with two friends to give his widow an annuity till her death.[2] If Wilberforce did not meet John Wesley often, he knew of his work and admired his character. The great letter of encouragement which John Wesley sent to him was indeed the last one he ever wrote (February 24, 1791). It showed the sustained interest of Wesley in the cause of abolition. He was not able to unbuckle his own armour without stopping to bless his successor in the fight.

When the Committee for the Abolition of the Slave Trade was formed in 1787 he wrote a letter warmly approving their aims. He warned them to expect difficulties and great opposition from those with vested interests. He said they were very powerful and would employ hireling writers who would show neither mercy nor justice. He said he would bring out a new and enlarged edition of his *Thoughts on Slavery* and he promised to speak favourably of the new Committee in the preface. He wrote a second time to them later and advised them on the right way to procure evidence. Thomas Clarkson, who reported the correspondence in some detail, seemed gratified that the Committee should have secured his distinguished support.[3]

Wesley was associated with another leader in the movement. On October 11, 1787, he wrote a fine letter to Granville Sharpe denouncing the iniquity of the traffic in slaves, and yet suggesting

---

[1] R. I. and S. W. Wilberforce, *Life of William Wilberforce*, p. 248.
[2] *ibid.*
[3] T. Clarkson, *History of the Abolition of the Slave Trade* Vol. I, p. 447.

THE AGITATION AGAINST SLAVERY

that a better means of information could be found than the hiring of paid informers.[1]

With Wilberforce, the greatest name of all, Wesley had most to do. Wilberforce was of course a staunch Evangelical, and had been greatly influenced by the ministry of John Newton. He never knew Wesley intimately but he showed a deep respect and even affection for him. After he had visited Wesley on February 24, 1789, he made the illuminating remark, 'What a fine old fellow.' Wesley on his side spoke of the 'agreeable' and 'useful' conversation, and thought Pitt was fortunate in having such a friend.

It was in the year following Wesley's death that the feeling against the trade in slaves reached its height. It was at this time that so many anti-slavery petitions were drawn up and sent to Parliament. Twenty-one Nonconforming bodies including Roman Catholics sent in petitions and secured a total 132,978 signatures. The Methodists, however, forwarded petitions with 229,426 names.[2]

Wilberforce opened the debate in the Commons on the abolition of the slave trade (April 2 and 3, 1792) with a masterly survey of the abominations of the slave trade. Then he proceeded to show the trade was not essential to the welfare of the planters. Fox in a magnificent peroration denounced the traffic, and Pitt on this occasion, speaking in support of the motion, delivered perhaps the finest speech in his career. The two opponents of the Bill were Baillie and Tarleton, recognized champions of the trade. Their speeches were not half so damaging as that of Dundas, who pleaded for moderation and asked that abolition should proceed gradually. Despite the eloquence and prestige of Pitt, the Revolution in France, and the awful rising of negroes in San Domingo, clouded the judgement of the Commons. The amendment of Dundas was carried.

The Commons agreed that the slave trade must gradually be abolished. When on April 23 and 27 the House discussed the exact date of abolition, it was fixed for the year 1796. Unhappily the motion approved by the Commons was thrown out by the Lords. The opportunity had gone and Pitt became absorbed in foreign affairs. The struggle with Napoleon precluded any further hope of getting the Bill through both Houses until there came a truce in

[1] *Journal*, October 11, 1787, note.
[2] Wesley's Studies by various writers, p. 190.

the war by the peace of Amiens. More than any other reason, the success of the last effort was due to the chance which brought Fox into power for a few short months after the death of Pitt. His coalition ministry had too many unstable elements to survive, but it lasted long enough for Fox to show his unremitting zeal in the cause of abolition. It was given to him, although a dying man, to set a seal upon the labours of Wilberforce.

Methodists had helped Wilberforce in the struggle of 1792. He had written a letter to the Methodist Conference, 1791, and sent them documents. The Conference, in return, wrote pledging him their hearty co-operation in his labours. This promise they fulfilled in the amazing number of names they secured for petitions.

In this last effort, the *Methodist Magazine* took its place with the *Evangelical Magazine*, and the *Eclectic Review*, as a doughty antagonist of the slave trade. In its pages Wilberforce was praised and his work commended.[1] Just before the Bill for the abolition of the slave trade came before Parliament, Wilberforce was threatened with the loss of his seat. Methodists who were influential in the city of York were alarmed at the prospect, and sent out the following circular:

York, October 20, 1806.

Dear Sir,

As a canvass has already begun for this County on the event of a general election we feel it right immediately to inform you that we feel it our duty to unitedly come forward in support of our present member, Mr. Wilberforce, who has on all occasions distinguished himself as a real friend of religion, and whose political sentiments and unwearied exertions to procure an abolition of the slave trade have endeared him to us and to our Society at large. We doubt not that your views on the subject and those of our friends in your Circuit will coincide with ours. If so, it would be well to recommend to the friends of Mr. Wilberforce to exert themselves in his favour without delay, as the supporters of the other candidates are using their utmost efforts. We think it proper to acquaint you that the canvass made here by the friends of Mr. Wilberforce is made in his own particular interest, distinct from that of the other candidates.

We remain, dear sir,
Yours most affectionately,[2]
(Here follow thirteen names.)

The election took place the following May. Wilberforce, the Hon. Henry Lascelles and Lord Milton were the candidates. It

[1] See especially the *Methodist Magazine*, April 1806.
[2] John Lyth, *Glimpses of early Methodism in York*, 1885, York.

was a strenuously contested election. Some days before the poll, a second circular was issued by the three Circuit ministers in York, Joseph Taylor, Joseph Drake and Daniel Isaac. They earnestly pressed for more subscriptions, and redoubled exertions, as Wilberforce's prospects seemed to them very doubtful.

On the eve of the poll, a third circular was issued. This contained a list of promised subscriptions, and a last exhortation to vote for Wilberforce and persuade others to do so. When the results were declared, Wilberforce was top of the poll, Lord Milton was next, with the Hon. Henry Lascelles less than two hundred votes behind. It is no exaggeration to say that a major reason why Wilberforce retained his seat was the untiring endeavours of Methodists in York to secure his election.

After the abdication of Napoleon and his retirement to Elba, the Conference of 1814 sent forth an important resolution:

'Resolved that a dutiful address be presented to His Royal Highness the Prince Regent in the name and on behalf of Conference assuring him of our loyal and affectionate attachment to his person and family and the Government of our venerable Sovereign expressing our gratitude for our own religious privileges and the restoration of peace among the nations of Europe and we earnestly entreat that His Royal Highness be pleased to use his utmost endeavours to prevent the threatened revival of the African slave trade, and to secure the immediate and universal abolition of that most inhuman and unchristian traffic.'

In the next year, 1815, the *Gazette* published as its leading Article the Address of the Methodist Conference to the Prince Regent:

'We cannot conceal from your Royal Highness that amidst the many occasions of congratulations and thankfulness which the late events have produced, there is one subject which we as Christians can contemplate with no other emotion than the deepest regret. We refer to that article of the treaty with France in which it appears that the influence of your Royal Highness has not obtained as yet the consent of the French Government to abandon the purpose of reviving the slave trade. The removal of that detestable traffic under any modifications or for any period however limited we most earnestly deprecate as a calamity of incalculable magnitude. ... We are anxious the question should undergo such further discussion in the approaching Congress at Vienna as may lead to that great consummation, the immediate universal and unqualified abolition of the slave trade.'

In the three periods of the struggle against slavery, Methodism produced three great champions. John Wesley was the hero in the first period and Richard Watson in the last period.

The great name linking the period of Wesley with that of Watson is the name of Dr. Thomas Coke. Coke had been a clergyman in the Anglican Church for some years before entering the Methodist Society. In 1797 he became President of the Conference, and he held the Presidency of the Irish Conference for many years. His title to fame lies in his arduous labours for Foreign Missions. To him more than to any other single person must be given the credit of establishing and developing the work overseas.

He made missionary journeys in the West Indies on five separate occasions. Whilst he journeyed from island to island he saw the conditions under which slaves worked. He had of necessity to be circumspect in the West Indies, but when he returned home he threw himself wholeheartedly into anti-slavery propaganda. His culture and his social status, quite apart from his great ability and devotion, made him an outstanding figure in the years following Wesley's death, and his advocacy of the abolition of the slave trade gave pungency and direction to the whole Methodist agitation. It was through his influence that the Conference of 1807 determined that none of its preachers employed in the West Indies should be at liberty to marry any person who had not previously emancipated by legal methods, all the slaves of whom they were possessed. The Conference, guided by Coke, required any preachers who had by marriage, or by any other way, acquired slaves, to take immediate and effective steps to emancipate them.

Methodist missionaries who worked in the West Indies were not able to declare their opposition to the traffic in slaves whilst they were in active work. Their invariable practice was to teach the slaves the duty of submission and of diligent labour for their masters. They took no part in the propaganda affecting the political order of the island where they lived. The result was that when an awful rising broke out in San Domingo in 1790 and spread to Dominica not a single member of the Methodist Society was found to be implicated although the most careful investigations were made.[1] It was impossible for the missionaries to act otherwise; even as it was, the planters regarded them with suspicion and hatred. In Jamaica, by an Act passed in 1802, Methodist preachers were persecuted and imprisoned, and although the Act was rescinded in 1804 a further Act was passed in 1807 which was

[1] Report of Commission (quoted in *Anti-slavery Monthly Reporter*, 1833, Vol. V, p. 342).

THE AGITATION AGAINST SLAVERY

aimed directly at the Methodist ministers. In varying degree each island had the same story of persecution to tell.[1]

There were, however, no restrictions on missionaries when they returned home. They gave most valuable information to the Parliamentary Committee of Inquiry. They spoke freely and frankly at public meetings. All of them were in favour of the abolition of the trade, and when this was accomplished, of slavery itself. In the demonstrations of 1830–1833 their speeches had great effect because they had worked amongst the very people whose cause they were pleading.

As early as 1817 Watson attracted the notice of Macaulay, who wrote to Hannah More (May 31, 1817): 'Our great meetings this year have certainly been better conducted than I have ever known them. . . . Watson, the Wesleyan Methodist, spoke with singular delicacy and feeling, and with a degree of good taste that would have done credit even to such a man as Reginald Heber. He is certainly both an able and honest man.'[2]

When the Anti-slavery Society was formed Bunting hastened to support it and he was followed by Watson. The two stood together in their denunciation of slavery.

It was his secretaryship of the Missionary Society which enabled him to understand the condition of the slaves in the West Indies. Missionaries wrote to tell him how awful was the plight of such slaves as professed Christianity. Some were flogged merely because they attended chapel. They were a suspected class.

Watson did more for the slaves by his platform speaking and his constant writing than has been commonly realized. It was under the leadership of Watson that the Methodist Conference of 1825 resolved that 'the slavery of negroes, this Conference considers to be one of the most heinous of public offences, the principles of which as a nation it becomes us heartily to renounce and the practice of which we are bound to discontinue as speedily as a powerful benevolent regard to the interests of those who are the subjects of this oppression will permit.' In 1830 the Conference guided by Watson decided to depart from its usual policy of abstaining from politics. Methodists were urged to use the election

[1] G. G. Findlay and W. W. Holdsworth, *History of Wesleyan Methodist Missionary Society*, Vol. II, 1921.
[2] 'Life and Letters of Zachary Macaulay' quoted by E. J. Brailsford, *Life of Richard Watson*, p. 78.

franchise to bring the system of negro slavery to an end. Methodism responded to the appeal and when a mammoth petition urging the immediate abolition of slavery was presented to the Parliament of 1833 it was signed by three hundred and fifty-four thousand Dissenters. Of this number two hundred and twenty-four thousand were Methodists.

When the Anti-slavery Society published its address to the people of Great Britain and Ireland the signature of Watson appeared with leaders such as Clarkson, Wilberforce and Macaulay.

The *Anti-slavery Monthly Reporter*, which was a main organ of the abolitionist movement in its later years, spoke highly of the work done by the Methodist Church. Watson organized great meetings over the country, culminating in a monster meeting at Exeter Hall. At that meeting Sir James Mackintosh and Daniel O'Connell gave Methodism the chief place in the fight against slavery. One incident will serve to show the ardour of Watson in the cause of abolition. When Michael Sadler and T. B. Macaulay were rival political candidates for Leeds in 1832, Watson urged Methodists to vote for Macaulay even though Sadler was a Tory and had Methodist affiliations. 'Methodists ought not to hesitate for a moment between the two candidates for Leeds, Macaulay and Sadler. The latter has never opened his mouth in Parliament against slavery. Macaulay is trained to abhor it. He has committed himself already in the House, and to his venerable father that sacred cause owes perhaps more than to any man. Minor politics are, with me, out of the question, and if you feel as I do, I should be happy if you would say as much for Macaulay as is consistent for us as ministers. You are quite at liberty to use my name.'[1] It is perhaps significant that Sadler, although a candidate with a fine public record of philanthropic work, was surprisingly defeated.

When Watson was dying he received a letter from Thomas Fowell Buxton requesting his advice. Prompted by the letter he wrote his last public message on behalf of the slaves.[2] It was the size of a moderate pamphlet and it vigorously declared his hatred of slavery as an affront to humanity and religion. When it had been despatched he summoned John Mason to his bedside. 'I am a dying man,' he said, 'but it is a privilege to have lived to see the time when the day of liberty begins to dawn.'[3]

[1] *Methodist Magazine*, November 1933, p. 647.
[2] E. J. Brailsford, *Life of Richard Watson*, p. 82.   [3] *ibid*.

It is a coincidence that in the case of Richard Watson and John Wesley their last public letters should be protests against the traffic in slavery. For both of them work on behalf of the slaves was an expression of their religious belief.

Apart from the three great leaders, it ought to be recorded that valuable work in the abolition of slavery was done by missionaries whose very names are now forgotten. They were not only instrumental in helping to abolish slavery but they did much to alleviate the lot of the slaves who came under their care. All slaves who attended Methodist meetings received religious instruction and were given rudiments of education. The Rev. J. Barry, before a Commission of the House of Commons, said that if all the slave population had been instructed as well as those under Wesleyan care the slaves might be considered equal to ordinary persons.[1]

The *Anti-slavery Monthly Reporter* declared that neither in Tobago nor Grenada were there any public institutions by which infants and adult slaves were instructed in religious principles. No Sunday Schools existed. The writer said that only the Wesleyan Methodists had given any instruction to the slaves of these islands.[2]

When the Rev. J. Curtin gave his evidence before the Commission on Slavery he said he had resided in Antigua for thirty years. The only religion he had found among the negroes was that given by the Moravians and the Methodists. In education the slaves were most deficient apart from those taught by Methodists and Moravians.[3]

Out of thirty-two thousand Methodist members in the West Indies in 1833, twenty-three thousand were slaves. This number, which did not include adherents loosely attached, meant that there were far more slaves in the Methodist Society than in any other Church. It was largely due to Methodism that when emancipation came, the expected horrors of licence and of violence did not happen. Instead there was on the whole an amazing quietness. Slaves accepted the new status of apprenticeship without demur, and in the vast majority of cases returned to their old masters.

Methodism exercised a civilizing and refining influence over large numbers of the slave population in the West Indies. It

[1] Report of Commission quoted in *Anti-slavery Monthly Reporter*, Vol. V, p. 342, 1833.
[2] *ibid.*, Vol. I, p. 68.
[3] *ibid.*, Vol. V, p. 300.

mitigated the hardness of their lot and strove untiringly to secure their final emancipation. Wesley and Coke and Watson were leaders in the movement, but behind them were unknown Methodists who laboured and sacrificed without stint. For on this issue the Methodist Church thought and acted with one mind and one purpose.

CHAPTER II

SIDMOUTH'S BILL, 1811

METHODISM increased greatly in the first years of the nineteenth century. During the same period the Church, despite the Evangelical Revival, remained almost stationary. This situation alarmed its loyal adherents. Public attention was drawn to the strength of Methodism and its continued progress by an outspoken article in the *Quarterly Review*, November 1810. Southey was popularly supposed to have been the author. The scant praise which was given only lent added weight to the severe attack. Methodism was criticized not only for its principles but its danger to the Church. The article undoubtedly alarmed people. At this time was published a return of figures which gave the number of preaching licences issued between 1780 and 1808, and the number of 'churches' licensed for the Church of England during the same period.[1] The contrast between the advance of Methodism and the scarcely perceptible progress of the Church was remarkable. It is significant that only a few months after the publication of these figures, and the article in the *Quarterly Review*, Viscount Sidmouth brought his Bill before the Lords. It was a Bill which required all dissenting preachers to be licensed and which restrained unlicensed preachers from preaching.

Sidmouth has been described by Harriet Martineau as 'narrow, vain, sensitive, reactionary and cruel.'[2] This shrewd estimate is borne out by his official record. His tenure of the Home Office was marked by short-sighted illiberal acts. He had a number of paid agents who kept him informed of the movements of the Luddites and later of Reformers.[3] It was a system abhorrent to those who cared for liberty. He approved the massacre at Peterloo, and was the author of the Six Acts which repressed the freedom of speech, and of the Press, and of public meetings. He opposed the Roman Catholic Emancipation Bill of 1829 and the Reform

---
[1] *New History of Methodism*, Vol. I, p. 402.
[2] Harriet Martineau, *Introduction to the History of Peace*.
[3] P.R.O. State Papers Domestic, 1811.

Bill of 1832. His career was that of a wholehearted Tory who disliked and distrusted democracy, and was determined to stamp it out by vigorous and repressive measures.

Sidmouth, as became a Tory, was also a devoted member of the Church of England. He disliked Dissenters in general, not only for their political opinions, but for their separation from the Church. Methodists, he disliked most of all. He disliked their emphasis on experience in the spiritual life; he disliked their class meetings, and he could not tolerate the system of local preachers. To him, it was repugnant for ignorant men to presume to preach to others.

From some of the correspondence he received about this time, one can see the immediate reasons which prompted him to introduce his Bill. A man called Sparrow, the chairman of the Stafford Quarter Sessions, had written to say that fifteen men, of whom nine were journeymen potters, had presented themselves, and were required to take the usual oaths to qualify as Methodist preachers. Ten of them declared they had no particular congregation. They also said their education was received from God, and they had no need of school learning. A clergyman, the Rev. John Nance, wrote to Sidmouth from Ashford to say that Methodist preachers did not confine their exertions to the propagation of opinions but were employed in defeating the labours of the clergy. He said that they called the Church catechism a heap of nonsense.[1]

When Sidmouth introduced his Bill in the House of Lords, he said it was of importance that 'not every person without regard to his moral character and intellectual faculties should assume the office of instructing his fellow creatures in their duty to God. . . . Abuse existed to a considerable degree in the self-appointment of improper individuals. For if any person, however depraved, ignorant and illiterate, appeared at the Quarter Sessions and claimed to take the oath of allegiance to his Sovereign and against Popery he was entitled to a certificate although there was no proof of his fitness to preach nor of his having any congregation requiring his ministerial services.' He declared that the object of his measure was 'to procure a clear declaration of law, to remove the erroneous interpretation adopted by magistrates in general and to prevent improper persons from office. Certain persons claiming these certificates were cobblers, tailors, pig drovers and chimney sweeps.'

[1] E. Pellew, *Life of Lord Sidmouth*, Vol. III, p. 43.

His recommendation was that no one should be granted a certificate whose form was not signed by six reputable house-keepers of the persuasion to which the applicant belonged.[1] In the conclusion of his speech he showed his fear of the encroachment of Methodism. He said that England was in danger of having a nominal established Church and a sectarian people.

There was nothing ostensible in the speech to show it was directed against Methodists. Sidmouth, himself, said it was a Bill intended to explain and render more effective certain Acts of the first year of the reign of King William and Mary and of the nineteenth year of George III. 'So far as the same relate to "Protestant Dissenting Ministers."'[2] Nevertheless the whole intent of the Bill was to strike a deadly blow at the local preachers of Methodism. These were the 'cobblers, tailors, pig drovers, and chimney sweeps' against whom he tilted his lance. These were the men who had no specific congregation requiring their ministerial services. Dissenting ministers and the regular ministry of Methodism did not come within the category specified by Sidmouth. They were able to preach without let or hindrance. His Bill was intended to prohibit the irregular and unordained laymen from preaching. Had his Bill passed it would have crippled the whole Methodist Society. The number of ministers was not nearly adequate for the pulpits of Methodism. In the smaller chapels of the towns and in the scattered country chapels the services were conducted regularly by local preachers. That was one reason why Methodism was able to build so many chapels throughout the land. In no Circuit was the number of ministers equal to the number of chapels. The measure of Sidmouth was therefore his bold attempt to resist the progress of Methodism and to limit its activities. From his point of view it strengthened the Church, damaged Methodism, and swept away a horde of unlettered preachers.

The curious feature of the whole matter is that he was able so effectively to allay the fears of Coke and Clarke. Before he introduced the measure he asked them to come to his house and see him. They were flattered by the invitation, and also by the implied suggestion that they were obviously the two representatives of Methodism whom one would wish to see as the leaders of that body. Coke, with all his magnificent qualities, was yet susceptible to the

[1] W. Cobbett, 'Parliamentary Debates,' May 9, 1811.
[2] *ibid.*

influence of Church and aristocracy. He was socially and financially of better standing than many of his brothers, and he moved with ease and delight among people of culture and refinement. Clarke had no social ambitions, but his politics and outlook were broadly speaking those of Sidmouth. The two men, then, came with a prejudice in favour of Sidmouth rather than a mistrust of him. Any fears they had were allayed, and they went back greatly charmed and relieved to their colleagues. These, however, were not so easily appeased. A meeting of the Committee of Privileges was hastily convened. At that meeting, the two most prominent laymen, Joseph Butterworth and Thomas Thompson, carried through a series of resolutions protesting against the Bill (May 14). A deputation was sent to Sidmouth with Thomas Thompson at its head. Sidmouth was courteous but refused to consider withdrawing his Bill. He confessed himself unable to see any cause for their alarm.

The next move lay with the whole Connexion. Meetings were held in all the principal towns and cities, and resolutions were passed petitioning Parliament against so intolerant a Bill.[1] In the course of a few days thirty thousand Methodists had signed petitions against the Bill.[2]

Sidmouth had moved the first reading on May 9 before the Methodist body could mobilize its forces. Even at the first reading, however, there was opposition. Lord Holland, in a vigorous speech, declared that being of inferior station did not make men inferior preachers. Social standing should not prevent people from preaching. Lord Stanhope also opposed the measure. Sidmouth knew that opposition would only grow stronger if there was a delay in the various readings of the Bill. He therefore gave notice that he was going to move the second reading of the Bill on May 21, which was the earliest possible moment. Even in this short time propaganda against the measure was so effective that when on May 21 the House of Lords considered the Bill, the Earl of Liverpool suggested that in view of the alarm created, the measure be dropped. He said five hundred petitions had been received, and some were signed by over a thousand people. Sidmouth declared that though the petitions might seem formidable, he knew of many Dissenters who were in favour of his Bill. Once again Lord Holland spoke eloquently and convincingly against the measure. He said the Bill was an infringe-

[1] J. W. Thomas, *Reminiscences of Methodism in Exeter*, p. 36, N.D.
[2] *Methodist Magazine*, p. 639, 1811.

ment of the natural right of the individual to interpret the Scriptures. Men, he said, were to be barred by having to seek six housekeepers to guarantee them. He said the whole body of Methodist itinerants would be exposed to peculiar hazard. Stanhope also spoke again, and said he hated the Bill because he loved liberty. Even those who supported the Bill, the Archbishop of Canterbury and Lord Erskine, felt that in view of the agitation, it would be wiser to drop it. It was obvious that the Bill had no chance of success. Sidmouth withdrew it without the House going into division.[1] It was a conclusive and spectacular victory for Methodism.

The Bill proved, however, to be the first battle in a campaign. Within a short time of its rejection, a circular was sent to the Quarter Sessions in different parts of the kingdom.[2] As a consequence, a new interpretation was given to the Toleration Act, and applications for licences on the old terms were rejected.[3] Many magistrates insisted that applicants should show they were ministers of separate congregations. At the Leeds Sessions in February 1812, several Methodist preachers were refused licences because they had no particular congregations of which they were ministers. The magistrates were strengthened in their decision by a verdict of the Court of the King's Bench, whereby it was held that a man desiring a licence to preach must show he had a particular congregation.[4]

Under these circumstances the Committee of Privileges felt once more called upon to act. It sent a deputation to Perceval and received his promise of support. It also issued a circular to the whole Methodist Society stating that it would lose no time in taking 'such measures as would be likely to promote the success of an application to the legislature for relief.' With the circular they enclosed a letter from Perceval who was then Prime Minister. Perceval promised to support such an application to Parliament and gave his consent for the letter to be published. Although Perceval was assassinated on May 11, 1812, the new Premier, Lord Liverpool, agreed to the wishes of the Committee. A Bill was drawn up which went through the two Houses and received the Royal assent on

[1] W. Cobbett, 'Parliamentary Debates,' May 1811.
[2] J. W. Thomas, *Reminiscences of Methodism in Exeter*, N.D.
[3] S. Drew, *Life of Thomas Coke*, p. 336, 1817.
[4] G. Smith, *History of Methodism*, Vol. III, p. 196, 1857.

July 29, 1812. Methodists felt that this new Toleration Act afforded liberty of worship, and secured to Englishmen the sacred rights of conscience.[1] The Bill did secure finally the right of local preachers to continue their preaching undisturbed.

The Conference of 1812 sent out a long manifesto to the superintendents of all Circuits. A short summary of the Conventicle, and Five Mile Acts was given, and then of the Toleration Act, which afforded protection to Dissenters. Conference declared that magistrates by putting a new construction on this Act had refused the oath to several applicants who were unable to show they had a particular congregation. In addition there were evidences over the country of hostility to preachers. The Press teemed with slanders against them. They were spoken of as 'vermin only fit to be destroyed.' Certain popular publications, said the Conference Address, called on the legislature, loudly and repeatedly, to adopt measures of coercion against Methodists. They pressed for the enforcing of the Conventicle Act, and Methodists felt their liberties seriously threatened. Since many Methodists were by principle attached to the Church of England, they could not conscientiously take oaths as Dissenters. The Committee of Privileges, therefore, felt no amendment of the Toleration Act would answer the case. They therefore worked on the principle 'that it is the unalienable right of every man to worship God agreeably to the dictates of his own conscience and that he has a right to hear and teach those truths which he conscientiously believes without any restraint or interference from the civil magistrate, provided he does not thereby disturb the peace of the community.' A Bill was drawn up embodying this principle and making Methodist religious worship known. Oaths were not to be taken as an antecedent qualification, but when required were to be taken before one neighbouring magistrate instead of the Quarter Sessions.

The Conference, in the last part of its manifesto, sketched the main provisions of the Bill which the Earl of Liverpool sponsored, and which had passed into law. This Toleration Act repealed the Five Mile and Conventicle Acts, and another Act which had injured the Quakers. It relieved of all penalties of the several Acts mentioned in the Bill, Protestants who resorted to a congregation specified in the Acts. No person need relinquish his attachment to the established Church in order to bring himself under the

[1] G. Smith, *History of Methodism*, Vol. III, p. 196, 1857.

protection of the Bill. If on the other hand a man was a Dissenter, he was still protected by the Act. All places of worship must be certified to the proper court, but a preacher need not wait till the place be registered before he preached. By former Acts only five persons could meet without the need of having the place registered, but now the number was extended to twenty persons. By former Acts no person could preach without taking the Oath, but by this, any person could preach without taking the Oath, until required to do so by the request in writing of one magistrate. No person was obliged to go to the Quarter Sessions to take the Oath. He could take it before one Justice and could not be compelled to travel more than five miles for the purpose. Unlike the Toleration Act, rioters who did not come inside the Church were punished equally with those who did, provided they made a disturbance which interfered with the service. The penalty of forty pounds was double the amount for rioting named in the Toleration Act. Lastly, by the Writ of Certiorari, proceedings could, if necessary, be removed to the Court of the King's Bench. The Conference manifesto concluded with thanks to the particular individuals who had facilitated the passage of the Bill.

A dangerous attempt to injure Methodism through the legislature one year and through the judicature the next had been successfully foiled. Methodism emerged from the ordeal stronger than before. There was, however, another way in which Methodism was attacked after the failure of Sidmouth's Bill. A most determined attempt was made to levy Poor Rates on chapels and meeting houses. An article in the *Gentleman's Magazine* (June 22, 1811) said it had been determined in the King's Bench that profits arising from the letting of pews, etc., in Methodist chapels should be subject to the Poor rate. Many chapels were assessed. The Methodist chapel in the Mint at Exeter actually had to suspend its weekday services, and for a time the chapel itself was closed because of its heavy assessment.[1] The trustees of Surrey Chapel appealed against their assessment, and their appeal was sustained. Poor rates were not levied and a valuable precedent was thus established. The Act of 1812 had favourable repercussions and this form of annoyance gradually disappeared.

Richard Carlile in one of his open letters declared that Sidmouth's memorable Preachers' Bill was an attempt to strike a fatal

[1] J. W. Thomas, *Reminiscences of Methodism in Exeter*.

blow at Methodism. When it failed the Government realized the great power of Methodism in the country, and the seat Butterworth gained at Dover was a proof of the value the Cabinet set upon the influence of the Methodist Society.[1] Carlile wrote as a bitter enemy and there is no indication that Butterworth's seat at Dover was a Government peace offering, but the general contention is indisputable. Methodism had been known to have a wide religious constituency. After 1811 there was no doubt about its strength, and its influence on the whole life of the nation. Not again did the Government by any measure cause a most powerful ally to become an unwilling foe.

[1] *The Republican*, Vol. III, September 19, 1823.

PART III

METHODISM AND THE MOVEMENTS OF THE PERIOD

CHAPTER I

THE INDUSTRIAL REVOLUTION

METHODISM had an excellent opportunity of being the Church of the Industrial Revolution. The period of its rise was roughly coincident with the rise of industrialism. It affected the same areas and reached the same classes of people. It was able to profit from the conservatism of the Church and its close connexion with the land. The strength of the Church lay in the South. There was not a single Bishop in Lancashire, or the West Riding until 1836 when the Bishop of Ripon was appointed. Manchester had to wait until 1847. Leeds until the middle of the nineteenth century was one parish of 150,000 people. The parochial organization of the Church was practically the same as at the Reformation. It was therefore adapted to a country which drew its wealth from the land and from commerce, but not from industry.

One of the features of Methodism was its extreme mobility. In the slow transformation of England from a pastoral to an industrial community, John Wesley was able to traverse the country many times on horseback. Later the work needed not a man but a system; not an Evangelist but an Evangelical Society. It was the happy fortune of Methodism to have begun in an age when a few devoted leaders could make a deep impression on the country, and to have become an organized Society at a time when England had become an industrial community. It was due to the genius of Wesley as an administrator that Methodism, even when highly organized, did not lose its mobility.

Wesley was not content to be the sole itinerant. All his preachers were 'travelling preachers': the whole system was one of itinerant preaching. Amongst his famous 'Twelve rules of a helper,' was the injunction, 'Go not to those who need you but to those who need you most.' He felt that a year was ample time for a man to stay in one place. Wesley believed a preacher could not keep his freshness and persuasiveness in preaching after such a period. Consequently, his preachers travelled incessantly and evangelized parts of England which had hardly been touched. The rough colliers of Kingswood and Newcastle, the tin miners of Cornwall, the new urban populations of Lancashire and Yorkshire were all deeply influenced by Methodism. Thus the strength of the Society lay in the industrial area.

There were, however, other reasons why Methodism might easily have become the Church of the Industrial Revolution. The architecture of the chapels was simple and homely, and the service was free from ritual and easy to understand. The preaching was plain, practical and experimental. It was well calculated to appeal to the new populations who had in large measure drifted outside the pale of the established Church.

The Reformation inspired an outburst of religious lyrical poetry and music. The hymns and tunes of sixteenth-century Germany rank among the finest of any age. Calvin insisted on metrical psalms alone, and when Calvinism reached Scotland, it brought a love of psalm-singing which has never languished. In England, the Elizabethan period was the golden age in music as well as literature. Refugees who had fled from the country during the persecution of Queen Mary came back from the continent with new settings for the Psalms, including the world-famous 'Old Hundredth.' Meanwhile, Sternhold and Hopkins in England had prepared a metrical version of the Psalms, which in the next century contended with the version of Tate and Brady for popularity.

Despite the fact that some of the best common-metre tunes were composed in this period, it was still a serious limitation to be restricted to metrical paraphrases of the Psalms. Emancipation came through the hymns of Isaac Watts (1674–1748). He had an extraordinary facility for writing sacred poetry. Like Pope, he 'lisped in numbers for the numbers came.' His *Horae Lyricae* (1706), *Hymns* (1707), *Psalms and Hymns* (1719) and *Divine and Moral Songs for Children* (1720) are landmarks in English Hymnology. He took not the Psalms but the whole Bible for his material. Indeed, some of his noblest hymns owe their inspiration not to any Biblical passage but to the mystery and grandeur of life itself. He wrote much verse that was bad, but at his best he ranks with Charles Wesley.

Isaac Watts broke down the barriers which had been imposed on singing.[1] It was left to Charles Wesley to make fullest use of this

---

[1] Mention ought to be made of the hymns of Philip Doddridge (1702–1751).

new freedom. His hymns are the finest expression of the evangelical doctrine of the faith. He issued many collections of hymns during the century, and the Hymn Book of 1780, which became the standard book of the Society until 1874, was composed almost wholly of his hymns, and some of Isaac Watts, together with the great translations from the German of John Wesley.

Hymns occupied an important place in the Methodist service, which meant that the laity took a prominent part in the service. They were able to sing to good musical tunes the lyrical poetry of Charles Wesley. It was so novel and so exhilarating an experience that Methodism easily outstripped other religious bodies in its hold over the industrial population.

Gradually, however, the early advantage was lost. Methodism ceased to attract the worker and to inspire his confidence. The Industrial Revolution was allowed to work out blindly its own destiny, uninfluenced by religious considerations. It was in a sense the tragedy of Methodism that having accomplished so much, it was not able to accomplish more.

There were certain main factors which prevented Methodism from being the Church of the Industrial Revolution. It has been pointed out that the medieval theologians interpreted 'calling' to mean the state of life in which the individual has been set by heaven.[1] Even Luther did not depart from this usage of the word. Men were not encouraged to leave the trade in which their family was engaged, nor to seek a higher station than that into which they had been born. In the Middle Ages a man might rise within his trade guild from apprentice to master. Occasionally it was possible in this way for a Dick Whittington to become Lord Mayor of London. Otherwise advance in life came through being a Jew,[2] or through a career in the Church. Even to-day, it is Protestant, and not Catholic, countries that are prominent for big business and capitalistic enterprise.

Calvin gave the word 'calling' a different connotation.[3] For him it meant the strenuous endeavour of the individual to achieve greater success. In England Calvinism meant the rise of modern

[1] Max Weber, *The Protestant Ethic and the Spirit of Capitalism*, 1930.
[2] The Jew was debarred from holding Public Office, but not from some forms of business.
[3] Max Weber, *The Protestant Ethic and the Spirit of Capitalism*, 1930, p. 3. Cf. R. Tawney, *Religion and the Rise of Capitalism*.

commerce. The virtues which it extolled had direct economic value. Honesty, sobriety and industry were good both in business and religion. The sturdy individualism of Calvinism, which set store on initiative and perseverance, and bade a man make his calling and election sure, marked the beginning of Capitalism. The very austerity of Calvinism which prevented a man spending his money on alcohol, or the theatre, or the gaming tables, stimulated habits of thrift and frugality. The conception of the world as evil limited the activities of the individual and enabled him to apply himself with concentration to his business.

Superficially it might seem that Methodism did not share this Calvinist tradition. The theology of Methodism was opposed to Calvinism on the fundamental issue of the extent of God's grace to man. Methodism, unlike Calvinism, was primarily a theology of experience. Whilst, however, it had this strong emotional basis, it laid emphasis on experience showing itself in conduct. Wesley was always concerned that faith should issue in good works. Antinomianism was the heresy against which he directed his most pointed barbs.

Wesley shared Calvin's distrust of the natural man. His sermons on 'Public Diversions' and on the 'Reformation of Manners' are diatribes against fashionable amusements. Sloth, luxury and indulgence, he attacked in more than one pamphlet.[1] His sermons on 'Friendship with the World' and 'In what sense we are to leave the World,' limited the intercourse of Christians and non-Christians to the barest civility. He discouraged Methodists from meddling with politics, save to support the candidate who feared God, and honoured the King and Constitution. The only realm left was the world of business, chapel and family. The chapel was the social as well as the religious centre for Methodists, and business was otherwise the dominant interest of life. To it he brought a boundless capacity for hard work. Wesley never tired of insisting on the importance of using every moment of time to fullest advantage. He said that in the affairs of life all a man's wisdom, all his resolution, all his patience and constancy were necessary.[2] He could not have described more succinctly the qualities necessary for material advancement. Beyond question, Methodism, so far as business life

[1] *Thoughts upon Dissipation, Manners of our present time*, 1783. *Thoughts on the present Scarcity of Provisions*, 1773.
[2] Sermon LI, 'The Good Steward.' *Works*, Vol. VI, p. 149.

was concerned, followed the Calvinist tradition. The words of Wesley on the conduct of a business man are clear and emphatic. He said it was the bounden duty of all who were engaged in worldly business to observe that first and great rule of Christian wisdom with regard to money.

'Gain all you can. Gain all you can by honest industry. Use all diligence in your calling. Lose no time.... Every business will afford some employment sufficient for every day and every hour. That, wherein you are placed, if you follow it up in earnest will leave no time for silly unprofitable diversions. You have always something better to do, something that will profit you more or less. Whatsoever thy hand findeth to do, do it with thy might. Do it as soon as possible. Do not sleep or yawn over it. Put your whole strength in the work. Spare no pains. Let nothing be done by halves, or in a light and careless manner. Let nothing in your business be left undone, if it can be done by labour and patience.... Gain all you can by common sense, by using in your business the understanding God has given you. It is amazing to observe how few do this: how men run on in the same dull track as their fathers.... It is a shame for Christians not to improve on them, whatever he takes in hand. You should be continually learning from the experience of others or from your own experience, reading and reflection to do everything to-day better than you did it yesterday.... Make the best of all that is in your hands.'[1]

The inevitable consequence of this teaching was that Methodists prospered. It was a process which greatly worried Wesley. He saw his Society becoming prosperous with all the attendant perils of prosperity. Repeatedly, and in the strongest language, he inveighed in his later years against the love of money and the danger of riches.[2]

When he died in 1791 Methodism was becoming middle class in social status. The leaders of the local Societies were often men of position and wealth. Consequently Methodism was able to stand the strain of building the chapels which began to rise throughout the Kingdom. Writing to the *Westminster Journal* as early as 1761 John Wesley said he could not believe religion had in any way hurt the circumstances of tradesmen. He said he knew of a hundred tradesmen in London who began to be industrious when they feared God, and their circumstances low enough until then, had become easy and affluent. He went to Macclesfield in April 1787,

[1] Sermon L, 'The use of Money.' *Works*, Vol. VI.
[2] Sermons on 'The Danger of Riches.' 'On Riches.' 'On Worldly Folly.' 'On the Danger of Increasing Riches.' *Works*, Vol. VII.

and found a people 'still alive to God in spite of swiftly increasing riches.'[1]

A Methodist writer, who claimed an extensive knowledge of manufacturing areas, stated that many factories were owned by Methodists and in many cases Methodists were chosen as foremen and overlookers.[2] In this same year, the Wesleyan Conference, in its Pastoral Address, spoke of an undue attachment to worldly business on the part of many Methodists.[3] A writer who was far more unbiased than the usual critic of Methodism wrote in 1804 that 'several people of property and genteel education make at present a part of the Methodist body.'[4] He proceeded to say that the generality of its members were still poor.

It is easy to understand what happened. The people of wealth and influence were no doubt in the minority, but their position gave them an importance out of all proportion to their numbers. The Methodist point of view was that of its wealthy middle-class adherents. In many chapels the wealthy trustees were opposed to the administration of the Sacrament, except by men episcopally ordained. They were supported by certain ministers prominent among whom were Benson, Vasey and Rodda. So great was the influence of these wealthy laymen that at one time local control of the chapels seemed a distinct possibility.[5]

One indication of the changed outlook was the institution of pew rents. In Wesley's day the gospel was free for all who came, but just before his death rents were charged for sittings in the chapels. At first it was done in the larger town chapels but it soon became general. The practice brought a stinging pamphlet from an aggrieved person who wrote: 'Chapels are now conducted too much on the same system as those haunts of Satan, the playhouses. No one is admitted who can't pay or who has not a ticket. I expect soon to see regular chapel bills published stating the nature of the performance and concluding with "Admittance to the Galleries. Places to be taken off Mr. —— Deacon, at the Pew Office." ... In Seafields not long since a gentleman was stopped by a doorkeeper who told him he could not pass without a ticket. "I thought the

[1] *Journal*, April 3, 1787.
[2] Joseph Sutcliffe, *The Review of Methodism*, 1805.
[3] *Arminian Magazine*, 1805, p. 524.
[4] *Stricture on Methodism*, by a Careful Observer, 1804.
[5] Abel Stevens, *History of Methodism*, Vol. III, p. 36, 1875.

THE INDUSTRIAL REVOLUTION 91

gospel was free to all," said the gentleman, "but pray how much is a ticket?" "Half a crown," said the doorkeeper. The gentleman walked away.'[1]

The writer of the pamphlet went to a large chapel near St. James's Square, and after standing a long time without anyone offering him a seat, he saw a board with the following notice: 'It is expected that those who have attended at this chapel a sufficient time to ascertain whether they like the preaching, do take tickets as they cannot be accommodated with seats without them.'[2] That the practice was not confined to larger chapels is shown in the history of Rothwell. The writer said that in 1822 the whole population was only 2,155, and yet the income from pew rents in the Methodist chapel was £32 11s. 9d.[3] It was the custom when a chapel was opened to reserve the majority of seats for pew-holders, and to allow a small number of seats to be free to the general public. At the opening of Leeds, Brunswick, a thousand out of the two thousand seats were left free, but these were reduced later.[4] Wilson, in his standard book on the Dissenting Churches of London, spoke of the area of a Methodist building 'filled with seats and pews: the galleries are allotted in the same manner, and seats are let out to the public by annual or quarterly tickets. As these places are made objects of profit, those who cannot pay for seats are crowded into a narrow space, and obliged to hear standing.'[5] Chapels came to depend on pew rents for the major part of their annual income. The whole system of pew rents meant the gradual alienation of the worker.

By the end of the eighteenth century the Methodist Church whilst still increasing greatly in numbers, and attracting artisans and workmen, had ceased to be the Church of the worker, and was controlled by respectable middle-class people of strong loyalist views. The leading ministers with few exceptions had Tory affiliations: some such as Coke, Benson, Jabez Bunting, John Stephens, and Daniel Isaac were most outspoken in their Toryism. A most pungent criticism of this attitude was written by a radical in 1822.

---

[1] *Confessions of a Methodist*, by a Professor, 1810.
[2] *ibid.*
[3] J. Batty, *History of Rothwell*, 1877.
[4] J. Everett, *Memoirs of W. Dawson*, 1842.
[5] W. Wilson, *History and Antiquities of the Dissenting Churches*, Vol. IV, p. 560, 1804–1814.

He spoke of the material change which had come over Methodism. 'Preachers amalgamate with the richer and higher ranks of Society. Too often unjust plunderers are the honoured associates of the Methodist parsons, and from them he ventures not to dissent: but encouraged by their smile he joins the war whoop against Reform. He tells his flock it is the will of heaven they should be starved to death and be content.'[1] Thomas Thompson and Joseph Butterworth, the two Methodist Members of Parliament, though sitting as Independent members, voted in the Tory interest.

Perhaps the factor which most influenced opinion and alienated the mass of the new industrial population from Methodism, was the lack of sympathy with working-class aspirations. The dislike Methodism showed of the Luddites, and its bitter opposition to the political Reform meetings in the North, were not forgotten. Methodism frowned on all combinations and unions of working men, and refused to intervene when the Tolpuddle labourers were arrested for joining a trade union, even though six of the seven were Methodists and two were local preachers. This also was not forgotten.

Richard Carlile spoke for more than himself when he said that, 'the system of the day makes one part of the community rich and the other poor. Methodism supports the evil part of the system.'[2]

The final factor which lost for Methodism the support of the working classes was its undemocratic organization. The laity had no real choice in Church government though it is true that Dr. Bunting did fight for, and secure the right of the laity to sit on certain Committees. Preachers were supreme in their own chapels, superintendents over the Circuit, and the Conference (representative of preachers) over the whole Connexion. It was this feature more than any other which resulted in the various secessions from Methodism. Wealthy leaders of the local chapels exercised no doubt a powerful influence over their own Societies, but they had no official place in the constitution of Methodism. The class meeting and the system of local preachers were democratic elements in Methodism, but they did not affect the government of the Society by ministers. Ebenezer Elliott, the Corn Law Rhymer, who was

[1] *A New Year Gift to Wesleyan Methodism*, 1822. Cf. also *The Rise, Progress and Influence of Wesleyan Methodism*, 1831.
[2] *The Republican*, Vol. VIII, September 19, 1823.

one of the leaders in the agitation against the Corn Laws, and in the Chartist movement, ended one of his poems with these biting words:

> 'Ask ye if I, of Wesley's followers one,
> Abjure the home where Wesleyans bend the knee,
> I do—because the spirit there is gone
> And truth and faith and peace are not with me
> The hundred Popes of England's Jesuitry.'[1]

By the time of the Chartist agitation the breach of Methodism with the working classes was complete. Even in Durham, where Methodist influence had been so strong, party slogans began to replace Bible texts on the Union banners.[2] The growing interest in politics and the development of secular education encouraged a radicalism which owed nothing to religious inspiration. Organized religion was looked on as the friend and ally of the Capitalist system. Free thought was associated with radical Reform. Reformers began to trace their spiritual ancestry through Robert Owen to Paine and Godwin, Rousseau and Voltaire.

If the Methodist Church thus failed to hold the workers, there were from the outset individual Methodists who became leaders in working-class movements. The Primitive Methodist Church was in itself a protest against the autocracy of Wesleyan government and its conservative methods. It supplied through its local preachers many leaders of radical reform. It is significant that during the Chartist agitation Primitive Methodism with its wide political sympathies, doubled its membership. Throughout the century, even after Primitive Methodism had lost its former hold, Methodists came into public life as the spokesmen of the worker.

It is, I think, not just to blame Methodism for not giving to working-class schemes of reform, a religious impulse. The Methodist Church never attempted to formulate a political and economic policy. It conceived its mission to be along wholly different lines. It believed it had been raised up to save people from their sins and to bring them into a new relationship with God.

John Wesley preached salvation, and a possibility of Christian perfection, for each individual. All political philosophers in the eighteenth century had started from the idea of man's first inno-

---

[1] H. V. Faulkner, *Chartism and the Churches*, 1916, N.Y.
[2] E. Welbourne, *Miners' Union of Northumberland and Durham*, p. 370, 1923.

cency and simplicity of life. They believed his troubles had come since he contracted himself into society. But whereas they believed his salvation to lie in a reconstructed society, Wesley believed it to lie in a regenerated will. They spoke of the general will of society; he spoke of the new man in Christ Jesus. Wesley believed that the only function of the State was to remove hindrances from the free expression of individual effort.

He adopted this view because he had seen what possibilities of development lay in the most unlikely individual. He had seen the dissolute colliers of Kingswood and Newcastle, and the tin miners of Cornwall become sober and industrious communities. He was always in contact with men who under the influence of religion had become changed in habits and outlook. He saw those who had been idle and careless, rise rapidly to positions of trust and responsibility. It is no matter for surprise that he believed the whole face of society could be changed by the redemption of the individual.

This individualism of Wesley had its limitations. He believed that a changed man would change his environment, he did not consider whether a changed environment might not help to change a man. There is no protest in his writings against the evils of industrialism, there is no plea for the pauper, nor for the debtor, nor for the orphan. He did not sufficiently account for the way in which many were handicapped from the start. The poor, especially if workless, the feeble, the aged and the sick, were not able always to struggle and achieve by dint of their own efforts.

Wesley did realize, however, the value of self-reliance and individual initiative. Methodism made no small contribution to the Industrial Revolution when it gave to great numbers a new purpose and a new sense of responsibility. A writer in 1805 said that if anyone made a tour of the manufacturing districts he would find almost as many chapels as villages, and he would find each chapel crowded with attentive hearers. As a result of his tour he would discover that the commerce of the country was being conducted principally by persons attached to the Evangelical truth in one form or another.[1] When Methodism influenced the population of industrial and manufacturing areas, and the artisans and small traders of towns and villages, it did not merely change the character of such people. A change in character meant a change in habits. Money that was spent on drinking, gambling and other amusements was spent more

[1] Joseph Sutcliffe, *Review of Methodism*, p. 36, 1805.

freely on the necessities of life. This benefited greatly the trade and manufactures of the country. It was not industry alone that benefited. Workers who had increased their purchasing power, and gained wisdom in expenditure, were themselves profited.

It is not wholly accurate to say that the only way in which Methodism met the challenge of industrialism was by its doctrine of salvation. If Wesley formulated no theory of economics, he had a philosophy of wealth.

He believed that Methodists should gain all they could and he also urged them to save all they could; but he emphasized most strongly, the need to give all they could.[1] He forgot that whilst his first two injunctions appealed to a most powerful human instinct, his last and, to him, most important command, made no such appeal. No one, he said, should want more than he can use. He considered that those who loved money fell into temptation and the snare of hurtful desires. 'Who of you desires to have more than plain necessaries and conveniences of life! Stop! Consider! What are you doing! Evil is before you! Will you rush on the point of a sword? By the grace of God, turn and live!'[2]

He counselled men to provide for themselves and their families, and then he urged them in strongest terms to give to the household of faith and afterwards to all men. He interpreted this in the most literal terms. 'You who receive five hundred pounds a year and spend only two hundred pounds, do you give three hundred pounds back to God? If not, you certainly rob God of that three hundred pounds. . . . O leave nothing behind you!'[3]

He followed out his own advice strictly. He said that when forty-two years before he had desired to furnish poor people with cheaper, shorter and plainer books than any he had seen, he wrote many tracts generally at a penny a piece, and afterwards several larger ones. These had a greater sale than he could have thought possible, and consequently he had become rich unawares. But he protested that he neither desired it nor sought it, and when riches came he gave them away. 'I cannot help leaving my books behind me whenever God calls me hence; but in every other respect my own hands will be my executors.'[4] This of course actually happened. When he

[1] Sermon on the 'Danger of Riches.' *Works*, Vol. VII. p. 9.
[2] *ibid.*, p. 8.
[3] *ibid.*, p. 362.
[4] *Works*, Vol. VII, p. 89.

died he possessed a few pounds and his books. He had given away £30,000, and throughout his life had lived on the barest minimum, consistent with health.

But although Wesley cheerfully followed out what he believed to be the Christian teaching on wealth, his followers found it more difficult. Early Methodism was distinguished by its boundless philanthropy. Many approximated to Wesley's rigorous standards, but some years before he died, he found to his dismay and sorrow, that his advice was being disregarded. Methodists gave, but not with the open-handed liberality that he desired.

It was indeed a counsel of perfection. Had it been possible for the men who made fortunes out of the new industrial order to have disposed of their wealth in the way Wesley deemed essential, the evils of Industrialism would have been avoided. As it was, the Industrial Revolution was cursed by that very lust for wealth which Wesley so insistently denounced. Even his followers only imperfectly accepted his philosophy of money. It could not be expected therefore, that men uninfluenced by religion, would be moved by Wesley's pleading. It was a solution and a thoroughly effective one, but unhappily too idealistic in a society which did not contain a single other Wesley. There is something at once splendid and tragic in a sermon on riches he preached towards the very end of his life.

'Go to now, ye rich men! Weep and howl for the miseries that are coming upon you—that must come upon you unless prevented by a deep and entire change! . . . O how pitiable is your condition! And who is able to help you? You need more plain dealing than any men in the world and you meet with less. For how few dare speak as plain to you as they would to one of your servants! No man living, that either hopes to gain anything by your favour or fears to lose anything by your displeasure. O that God would give me acceptable words and cause them to sink deep into your hearts. Many of you have known me long, well nigh from your infancy. You have frequently helped me when I stood in need. May I not say you love me? But now the time of parting is at hand. My feet are just stumbling upon the dark mountains. I would leave one word with you before I go hence: you may remember it when I am no more seen.

'O let your heart be whole with God! Seek your happiness in Him and Him alone. Beware that you cleave not to the dust. This earth is not your place. See that you use this world as not abusing it: use the world and enjoy God. Sit as loose to all things here below, as if you were a poor beggar. Be a good steward of the manifold gifts of God, that when you are called to give an account of your stewardship He may say, "Well done, thou good and faithful servant, enter thou into the joy of thy Lord." '[1]

---

[1] Sermon 'On Riches.' *Works*, Vol. VII, p. 222.

Apart from his views on riches, Wesley had a conception of the relationship that ought to exist between master and men, which would have materially influenced the course of the Industrial Revolution. He derived from his religious beliefs, the essential kinship of men: no man was less impressed by money or social rank. He held as part of his creed the equality of all men's souls in the eyes of God.

He believed further in the Christian idea of stewardship. He was never weary of insisting on a man's responsibility to God for the things he possessed. The rich had a responsibility to the poor. When his immediate needs were satisfied, his money must be given to alleviate the sufferings of others. In each of his sermons on riches this idea recurs. His sermon on the Good Steward applied the principle of trusteeship to every part of life. The soul and mind and body must all be rightly used. Even here Wesley did not stop. He said that the Lord would inquire whether a man's advantages in person, address or knowledge, were used for promoting virtue in the world. He said that God would ask whether one's power or influence had been used for the increase of wisdom and holiness.

He believed that if, in industry, masters felt a responsibility for their workmen, and gave them a fair wage, and if they sold their commodities at a just price,[1] economic conditions would be transformed. He believed workmen ought to have a like sense of responsibility. They must give unstinted and devoted labour to their masters, regarding idleness as a crime. At a later date, William Arthur drew a picture of the type of Capitalist which Wesley had in mind. He described the career of a Methodist employer from its humble beginnings, and showed how his business had been built up by unceasing concentration, and by business integrity. His relations with his men had been so friendly that they gave him devoted service, and at his death lamented him as though they had lost a father. It was an attractive picture of the relationship between employer and workmen that Wesley desired to see.[2]

Wesley could not foresee the dimensions of the Industrial Revolution, nor realize how impossible were his ideas of a close personal relationship between master and men. It was not that his views of money or of human relationships were at fault but that they were

[1] 'We cannot sell below the Market Price.' Sermon on the 'Use of Money.' *Works*, Vol. VI.
[2] William Arthur, *The Successful Merchant*, 1835.

impracticable. The real indictment is that the whole emphasis was placed on regeneration and not sufficient attention was paid to reform. Oastler, speaking in 1833, declared that Wesleyan ministers in the North of England all knew of the ill-treatment of children in factories, and yet were quiescent.[1] It must be said in justice, however, that men were still far from the day when State interference was looked on as welcome and necessary. It was not until the second half of the nineteenth century that the influence of collectivism shaped legislation. State grants to Education, Employers' Liability Acts, the legislation of Trade Unions, all came on the Statute Book in this period. The beginning of the century has been described by an eminent Jurist as the period of old Toryism.[2] It was a time when the conservatism of men's thinking was strengthened by the deadly struggle with Napoleon and the fear of seditious propaganda at home. Legislation was reactionary and repressive, and reform was indefinitely delayed. Societies and clubs were driven underground, and combinations had no chance to exist. Out of this time, when the fear of men made them cruel, came the period of Benthamism, in which men only welcomed the interference of the State to remove restrictions on individual freedom. Men were to be left free in order to work out their own salvation.

John Wesley and his immediate successors should not be censured too harshly for an individualism which was common not to themselves alone, but to the age in which they lived. Their attitude to the Industrial Revolution was not without fault. But with all their limitations, Methodists did see the evil of exploitation. 'We are to gain all we can without hurting our neighbour: this we cannot do if we are to love our neighbour as ourselves. We cannot if we love everyone as ourselves hurt anyone in his substance. We cannot consistent with brotherly love sell our goods below the market price: we cannot study to remove our neighbour's trade in order to advance our own: much less can we entice away any of his workmen. None can gain by swallowing up his neighbour's substance, without gaining the damnation of Hell.'[3] The whole teaching of Methodism was a condemnation of economic greed and selfishness. Methodists did appreciate the need for co-operation and

---

[1] G. J Holyoake, *Sixty years of an Agitator's Life*, 1892.
[2] A. V. Dicey, *Law and Opinion in England*, 1905.
[3] Sermon L, 'The Use of Money.' *Works*, Vol. VI.

understanding. They desired a community of interest between employer and employed. It was left to a later age to implement these ideas, and in part measure, to make such aspirations effective in Law.

CHAPTER II

EDUCATION

THE narrow views on education held by Wesley were adopted without question by his successors. Knowing his views on children and on education we know their attitude. The greatest of his followers, and one of the most enlightened, spoke of children as 'born in sin and shapen in iniquity.'[1] This was the view of total depravity stated in its baldest form. It involved the treatment Wesley advocated repeatedly and expressed in his written sermon 'On obedience to Parents.'[2] He said wise parents should begin to break the will of a child the first moment it appears. He declared that in the whole art of Christian education there was nothing more important than this. His argument was that the will of the child ought to be subjected to that of the parent. Children ought to be taught that in 'pride, passion and revenge, they are now like the devil; and that in foolish desires and grovelling appetites they are like the beasts of the field.'[3]

That his followers shared his views is shown by the maintenance of his harsh and narrow rules for Kingswood School. Children were allowed no holidays. When parents took them from school, they took them away for ever. It was not until 1811 that there came the slightest modification. In that year Conference agreed the boys might visit their parents once a year only in the month of September.[4] In 1813, Conference declared that boys were to have a vacation of two months every two years. Time has been on the side of the boys, and generations that knew not Wesley have shown a wider tolerance and sympathy.

Notwithstanding the early severity of school discipline, credit must be given to Wesley for starting day schools in Newcastle and London, and in founding what has become a well-known public school. This original impulse to provide education for

---

[1] Jabez Bunting, 'Sermon on a Great Work Described,' 1805.
[2] *Works*, Vol. VII, p. 103.
[3] Sermon on 'The Education of Children,' *Works*, Vol. VII.
[4] *Minutes of Conference*, 1811, p. 122.

children, led ultimately to the establishment of many schools for the purpose of public school education.[1] There is in the life of Kay Shuttleworth a reference to the interest of Methodists in education. When the education clauses of the Factories Regulation Bill had failed, contributions were received from friends of the National Society amounting to £160,000, whilst £70,000 was received from Wesleyan Methodists.[2]

Another way in which Wesley fostered the growth of education was in the dissemination of cheap literature. His own pamphlets which ranged from a philosophical treatise on liberty, to a method of removing dew damp from coach glasses, were distributed unceasingly throughout the country. Mainly for the benefit of his preachers, he published a *Christian Library* of fifty volumes, and gave people in an abbreviated form some of the great masterpieces of ancient and modern literature. He published grammars of many languages, and a History of England, which have now only an archaic interest, but which did serve to give some people the only education they ever received. Wesley had a great zest for life, and was tremendously interested in the events of his day. He wrote often and well on the contemporary condition of society and the problems which confronted it. His restless mind and ready pen enabled him to write on all the outstanding events of the century, and his many pamphlets, published very cheaply, interested a great lay public in what had been the province of a few specialists. His work was carried on by the next generation, and the Book-Room, after the death of Wesley, still continued to make large profits from the sale of books and pamphlets. There was, however, no longer a stream of pamphlets on political, economic, and social subjects, issuing from the Methodist Press. That source had dried up, and instead works chiefly of a devotional interest took their place. It meant of course that the educational value of the Press was diminished.

The great contribution Wesley made to education was not only

[1] In the Minutes of 1921 Conference the following schools were mentioned as acquired by the Twentieth Century Fund, but not under the full control of the Education Committee: East Anglian School, Bury St. Edmunds; Kent College, Canterbury; Truro College; Rydal Mount; West Cornwall College, Penzance (Girls); Woodhouse Grove School; also Schools at Kent, Jersey, Queenswood, Leys, Cambridge, Queen's College (Taunton), Kingswood.

[2] Frank Smith, *Life of Sir J. Kay Shuttleworth*, p. 133, 1923.

in building schools nor in publishing cheap literature, but in promoting the spread of Sunday Schools. Methodists were concerned in the movement from the start. They adopted the idea with enthusiasm, and Wesley was continually astonished at the great increase of Sunday Schools, and their immense potentialities for good. Richard Carlile, an avowed atheist and a foe of Methodism, said that Bible Schools for youth were directed mainly by the Methodists.[1]

One reason for the amazing development of Sunday Schools within Methodism was the enthusiasm and encouragement of Wesley himself. In theory, he may have been narrow and severe, but in practice he loved children and was loved by them. Matthias Joyce, at that time a Papist, went to hear Wesley in Dublin, and afterwards said that what impressed him most was to see John Wesley stoop down and kiss a little child that sat upon the pulpit stairs.[2]

There are some delightful stories which illustrate Wesley's love of children. On one occasion he met so many of them in one company that he described them as an army. They surrounded him and it was a long time before he could regain his freedom. Once he collected a number of them, and took them into the house of his host and persuaded them to sing for him. At another time he filled his coach with them and for the space of an hour took them a ride around the town.

It is significant that after 1776 he no longer records in his *Journal* how he spoke to parents on the duty of instructing their children. Instead, there are constant references to his meeting with the children themselves.

The importance of these Sunday Schools was heightened by the fact that they provided the only education which many pupils received. The great public schools had by this time belied their name. The education provided was beyond the means of all but wealthy people. For the middle classes there existed Grammar Schools. Unfortunately the Grammar Schools at this time were few in number and in a state of great disrepair. It was not until the second half of the century that their importance was realized and a better use made of them. Dissenting Academies had been at one

---

[1] *The Republican*, September 18, 1819.
[2] Wakeley, *Anecdotes of the Wesleys*, p. 229. See also Matthias Joyce, in *Lives of the Early Methodist Preachers*.

time the University of the Dissenter. Men who could not go to the older Universities because of religious disabilities found in the Academies a high educational standard. Wesley's own father received part of his training in a Dissenting Academy. In time, however, there came a change in character and organization and their prestige fell. In any case there was never a time when the Academies were generally used and widely appreciated. After 1779 Nonconformists were allowed by law to teach, and a number of new private schools were started. These were designed to meet the needs of the sons of merchants and manufacturers.[1]

There were three main types of education offered to the poorer classes. The Society for the Propagation of Christian Knowledge had fostered the growth of charity schools which started in 1698. Education was of a most elementary nature. It was considered sufficient that boys and girls should be able to read and write. Afterwards, boys were apprenticed to a handicraft trade, and girls were sent out to menial service. At one time the schools were well attended, but by the close of the century their influence had greatly diminished.

In the second place, there were in all parts of the country Dames' Schools, so called because they were usually conducted by a spinster or a widow to eke out her pittance. The schools had a name for disorderliness, but no corresponding reputation for learning. In 1819, 53,000 children were being taught in these schools.[2]

In the third place, there were schools of industry which arose with the new Industrialism. They trained pauper children for industrial occupation but had only a limited usefulness. Out of 194,914 pauper children in 1819 who were between the ages of five and fourteen, only 21,600 enjoyed the benefits of elementary education in these schools.[3] Apart from the apprenticeship system which had only slight educational value, these were the three ways in which it was possible for poor children to be educated. In practice the majority received no education at all. The schooling of the century was totally inadequate. It was some years before the influence of Bell and Lancaster was strongly felt. That is why Sunday Schools were of such importance.

Sunday-school scholars were not often taught secular subjects

[1] H. McLachlan, *English Education under the Test Acts*, 1931.
[2] E. Halévy, *English People in 1815*, p. 400.
[3] *ibid.*

except indirectly, but they were taught to read, and the more intelligent would acquire a useful general knowledge. From the outset the schools had cultural value. Wesley claimed that they restrained children from vice and taught them good manners.[1]

The rate at which Sunday Schools increased may be gauged from the fact that in 1798 a Methodist Sunday School Society was started with a large number of children under its supervision. In 1805, 1,200 children were members of four Sunday Schools alone.[2] In 1823 there were in the London West Methodist Circuit 116 schools, 1,136 teachers and 15,073 scholars.[3] The increase in scholars was maintained so that by 1854 there were 401,763 children attending Wesleyan Methodist Schools, and the Wesleyan Conference of 1904 was able to report that over a million children were being instructed in Wesleyan Sunday Schools.

The hours at which the Sunday Schools were held, were exceptionally long. They covered the greater part of the morning and the afternoon. Bishop Porteous in writing to his clergy of Sunday Schools, said that in towns, four to five hours were sufficient for children, but more hours were possible in the country.[4] A writer complained that three masters were not sufficient to give lessons in a variety of subjects to eight classes of boys from morning till evening.[5] When the *Sunday School Teacher's Magazine* reported a typical Wesleyan Sunday School it gave the hours as 8.30 a.m. to 12, and 1.30 p.m. to 4 p.m. with no breaks allowed.[6]

The Methodists at York had three Sunday Schools with a thousand children and one hundred and forty-two teachers in all. Each School was arranged in six divisions. The first was taught the Bible, the second concentrated on the New Testament. The third and fourth were taught parts of the Sunday School Union's reading and spelling book. The fifth was taught monosyllables, and the sixth was taught the alphabet.

The school was arranged with benches on each side of a centre aisle. The classes formed two sides of a square so that each scholar might see the superintendent. Each class had a chalked line marked

[1] *Journal*, July 18, 1784.
[2] E. M. North, *Early Methodist Philanthropy*, p. 110, 1914.
[3] J. J. Graham, *Chronicles of a Century at King's Cross*, N.D.
[4] C. J. Abbey, *The English Church and its Bishops*, 1887.
[5] J. A. Wenderborn, *View of England towards the Close of the Eighteenth Century*, Vol. II, p. 3, 1791.
[6] *Sunday School Teacher's Magazine*, Vol. VI, 1835.

EDUCATION

on the floor, on which scholars placed their feet when standing to repeat a lesson. Each class was provided with a box which was used for depositing the reading books, class cards and pencils. Every class had an Assistant who was one of the scholars. In this provision is seen the influence of Bell's monitorial system. The number of children in the class varied from fifteen to twenty-five, and their names and attendances were recorded in a book. Teachers were required to show ability, punctuality, diligence and decided piety. The Assistant teacher, or monitor, was the first scholar in every class. His task was to prevent idleness and assist scholars in their lessons. The scholars were told to come with hands and faces clean, and with their hair combed. They were to hang up their hats and sit down quietly. They were to walk without making a noise to and from the school, and they were not allowed to loiter or play in the streets. If they absented themselves from the school without good reason, they were to receive such punishment as the Superintendent might think they deserved.

The Superintendent himself was fined threepence if not at the school punctually at the time appointed. If he was absent without proper cause he was fined a shilling. The same rule applied to teachers but their fines were less in amount.[1]

This school was probably more efficient than the majority but it was typical in its hours and lessons of a Wesleyan Sunday School. Indeed it is certain that in other denominations similar conditions applied. At the annual meeting of the Sunday School Society which was representative of all the Churches, it was reported that 27,365 spelling books, 6,605 alphabets on boards, 5,853 primers, 720 Bibles and 3,852 New Testaments had been distributed in the year.

There have been preserved in the Wesleyan Methodist Church at Oldbury, records of a visit made to the chapel in 1802 by the Rev. Thomas Taylor, who was President in 1796 and later in 1809. He wrote a commendation on the front page of the hymn-sheets which were used. The address ran:

'I have had an opportunity now for twenty years of observing the amazing utility of Sunday Schools, in London, Manchester and Liverpool and various other towns and villages, and I can speak with truth, that their salutary influence has been unspeakable. Multitudes of poor untaught children who used to spend the Lord's day in associating together,

---
[1] *ibid.*

prompting and instructing the other, the more grown-up the younger in vice and wickedness such as swearing, lying, pilfering and all sorts of mischief; but by the above humane institution are happily reclaimed, many of them have become very useful members of Society. And this more particularly so where all the teachers act from principle and bestow their labour gratis, as is done in all the Methodist Connexion. The children are taught to read and write, and likewise their morals are attended to: to be diligent and industrious, to behave with respect to their superiors: to avoid lying, stealing, speaking vain words, and to be true and just in all their dealings. But although the teachers teach gratis, yet considerable expense is unavoidable, as the rent of the room, benches, books, paper, pens, and ink, &c. Hoping the inhabitants of Oldbury and its environs will see the utility of this laudable design and do all in their power to support it.

T. TAYLOR, Birmingham, 1802.'

In 1811 another famous preacher, the Rev. Jacob Stanley, came to preach sermons in aid of the Sunday School. In his written appeal addressed to the friends of the rising generation he said:

A few generous individuals commenced a Sunday School at Oldbury in the year 1799 for the express purpose of educating children in the rudiments of the English language, and in promoting the moral improvement of the children of the poor. This they have uniformly done without any emolument. Yet this gratuitous institution is attended with considerable expense arising partly from the rent of the schoolroom, partly from the purchase of books and partly from presents which are bestowed as rewards of merit to promote the spirit of emulation. To assist in meeting this expense the founders of the institution have found it necessary to solicit the aid of a generous public. In the treasurer's statement for the year May 1810 to May 1811 the written report showed that on copy books, &c., and premiums to children £23 15s. 5d. was spent.

Not all people were convinced of the wisdom of writing in Sunday Schools. There were two able writers in particular who used their pen to condemn it. G. B. Macdonald denounced it as an impediment to devotion and worship.[1] Valentine Ward and Macdonald attacked the practice also on the grounds that unscrupulous employers were using it as the sole means for the education of their employees. Too often, said Valentine Ward, the Sunday Schools are used as a substitute for day schools.[2] He said of all Sunday Schools, Methodists were the worst offenders in the practice of writing, and it was a practice which ought at once to be abolished.

The Wesleyan Conference of 1814 actually forbade the teaching

[1] G. B. Macdonald, *Facts against Fiction*, 1832.
[2] *Observations on Sunday Schools*, by Valentine Ward, 1827.

of writing, and repeated the injunction in 1825, but the very fact that it was still being denounced by writers as late as 1832, shows that the jurisdiction of Conference over Sunday Schools was not established. The probability is that at the start, Sunday Schools were only loosely connected with the chapels. They were not necessarily on the same premises nor was the instruction provided strictly Methodist teaching. One reason given for the rapid increase of Wesleyan Sunday Schools was the ease with which children were admitted.[1] It led one writer to say that the schools though Wesleyan in theory were undenominational in practice.[2]

Conference only slowly awakened to the opportunities which Sunday Schools and the education of children presented. The Conference of 1820 decreed that weekly meetings for children should be established in every large town. Not until 1827 did Conference do more than advise the schools. In that year it drew up rules of management for schools. It was as late as 1837 before the Methodist Conference affirmed the necessity for a Sunday School at every chapel.[3] The association of a school with a particular chapel brought the Sunday Schools directly under Conference, and they became in the process centres of Methodist instruction.

When in 1837 Methodism began to build day and infant schools, the Sunday Schools had no further need to teach writing and spelling. It is reasonable to assume, that from that period onwards, Sunday Schools were limited to Scriptural instruction and the Wesleyan Day Schools provided secular education.

This was not universally the case. In colliery districts and in some manufacturing areas, when even day-school education was considered a luxury, the Sunday School persisted as a means of culture and instruction. A Royal Commission which was set up in 1842 to consider the condition of young persons in mines, reported that 'except in Northern mining districts where Sunday Schools and Methodism was powerful, a pagan darkness prevailed.'[4] In Durham, converted hewers sat side by side with their own children, learning to read in order that they might enjoy their Bible.[5] A Durham miner, writing of his early experience, said that

[1] *Gentleman's Magazine*, April 1807.
[2] See E. M. North, *Early Methodist Philanthropy*, 1914.
[3] *ibid.*
[4] C. R. Fay, *Life and Labour in the Nineteenth Century*, pp. 187–188.
[5] E. Welbourne, *Miners' Union of Northumberland and Durham*, 1923.

pew rent at ninepence a quarter was charged in the side galleries of the chapel, and the money thus raised was devoted to the provision of papers, pen and ink, for the writing classes of the Sunday School. He worked his six days in the pit and then went on the Saturday night to the chapel, and ruled the copy books and wrote headings for the writing lessons in Sunday School the following day. He said that a man who had attended a day school up to the age of ten years was counted fortunate. The Sunday School thus became a school for instruction in the ordinary subjects of reading, spelling and writing. He said that his mother, and father, and multitudes of other persons at that time, owed all their education to the Methodist Sunday School.[1]

Thomas Burt, the famous Labour Leader, declared in his autobiography that his attendance at a Methodist Sunday School had helped him greatly. He found that in comparison with other boys he was a good speller and a good reader. As the place in the class depended upon expertness in spelling he was able nearly always to take the top place.[2]

The conclusion is that in the first years of the nineteenth century, Methodist Sunday Schools were held throughout the morning and afternoon, and were only loosely connected with particular chapels. Apart from the Bible, the subjects taught included at least reading and spelling and writing. In some cases instruction in manners and deportment was given. As the schools became identified with particular churches, their hours of meeting were limited. Usually they were held for an hour before the morning service, and in the afternoon. The growth of secular education limited the scope of instruction in the Sunday Schools to the Bible and the Methodist Catechism. In certain areas, however, the Sunday School remained to the end of the century as a centre of elementary education.

The schools which Wesley established in London, Bristol and Newcastle, were but the forerunners of a great number of day schools which made Methodism in the last century rank with the Established Church as the greatest force for popular education in England. In 1841 Conference set up a committee on education, and outlined its duties. Schools were to use the authorized version of the Bible and the Wesleyan Catechism. They were also to em-

[1] George Parkinson, *True Stories of Durham Pit Life*.
[2] Thomas Burt, *An Autobiography*, 1924.

ploy the Christian Psalmody and the Wesleyan Hymn Book. On the other hand, sectarianism was to be avoided and children, whatever their religious denomination were to be admitted. It was decided that each school should act under the instructions of a local committee, but every teacher had to be a Wesleyan and be recommended by his superintendent minister. A further step was taken by the Conference of 1844 when £20,000 was proposed as the basis of a fund for educational purposes. From this time Wesleyan Day Schools were built with great rapidity. In 1837 there had only been nine Infant and twenty-two Day Schools, but the Conference of 1857 reported 434 Day Schools with an attendance of 52,630 scholars. At this time over 400,000 children were being taught in Wesleyan Sunday Schools. It will thus be seen that the contribution of early Methodism to education lay not in any new approach to childhood, and any consequent educational theory, but in the provision of education for classes otherwise ignorant and neglected.

CHAPTER III

ROMAN CATHOLIC RELIEF

JOHN WESLEY was no bigot. He claimed that no society was more free from doctrinal tests than his own. He only asked those who sought membership whether they sincerely desired to be saved from their sins. Even the preachers were not pledged to any rigidly defined standard of doctrines, but only to the evangelical doctrines of the faith. In their interpretation of these, they were to be guided by his *Sermons* and his *Notes on the New Testament*. To this day the Notes and Sermons are not intended to impose a system of theology on Methodist preachers, but 'to set up standards of preaching and belief which should secure loyalty to the fundamental truths of the Gospel of redemption.'[1]

One of his most effective sermons was on 'The Danger of Bigotry.' In his sermon on 'The Catholic Spirit,' he praised the man of catholic spirit, as one who gives his hand to all whose hearts are right with his heart. This he interpreted to mean, all who believe in the Lord Jesus Christ, who love God and man, who are careful to abstain from evil, and are zealous of good works.[2] There is no mention of Creed or Sacraments or Church government. On the contrary he explicitly said:

'I do not mean embrace my modes of worship or I will embrace yours. This is a thing which does not depend either on your choice or mine. We must both act as each is fully persuaded in his own mind. Hold you fast that which you believe is most acceptable to God and I will do the same. I believe the Episcopal form of Church Government to be scriptural and apostolical. If you think the Presbyterian or Independent is better, think so still and act accordingly. I believe infants ought to be baptized and that this may be done either by dipping or sprinkling. If you are otherwise minded be so still and follow your own persuasion. It appears to me that forms of prayer are of excellent use particularly in the great congregation. If you judge extemporary prayer to be of more use, act suitable to your own judgement. My sentiment is that I ought not to forbid water wherein persons may be baptized: and that I ought to eat bread and drink wine as a memorial of my dying Master. However, if you are not convinced of this,

---

[1] *Minutes of Conference*, p. 364, 1923.
[2] *Works*, Vol. V, p. 499.

act according to the light you have. I have no desire to dispute with you one moment upon any of the preceding heads. Let all these smaller points stand aside. Let them never come into sight. If thine heart is as my heart; if thou lovest God and all mankind—I ask no more. Give me thine hand.'[1]

These are noble words on Christian tolerance and charity. Wesley practised them in the conduct of his life. His relations with members of other denominations were uniformly friendly. Even when he was attacked by fellow Christians such as George Whitefield, Augustus Toplady and Bishop Lavington, he never wrote with rancour or reproach. He always sought conciliation and understanding. Nothing was allowed to rankle in his mind. When a scurrilous pamphlet had been circulated in the streets of Bristol, and his brother Charles in great indignation wrote to him asking him to defend his honour, he replied it was not worth while for 'when I gave everything to God I did not leave out my reputation.'

The Church with which he had least sympathy was that of Rome. He declared that the Methodist emphasis on Justification by Faith was itself sufficient to undermine the whole fabric of Romanism.[2] In his *Word to a Protestant* he indicated three points in which Methodism and Romanism were not in agreement. The first was the Catholic doctrine of merit whereby salvation could come through works and not through faith alone. Secondly, the Roman practice of praying to the Saints and 'worshipping images' was considered by Wesley to be sheer idolatry. Lastly, Wesley objected to the persecuting principle which he believed to be inherent in Romanism. He uttered his strongest denunciations against the doctrines of the primacy of Rome, purgatory, and transubstantiation.[3]

These grave differences of belief did not make him uncharitable in his dealings with Catholics. In his *Letter to a Roman Catholic*, he stressed the points upon which both of them were agreed and made a strenuous plea for mutual understanding. He asked that there should be a mutual resolve not to hurt one another or do anything unkind or unfriendly to each other. He asked in the second place that they should not speak harshly or unkindly of each other but use the language of love. Then they were to avoid

---

[1] *ibid.*
[2] *Journal*, Vol. II, p. 262, August 1739.
[3] 'Roman Catechism.' 'Advantage of the Church of England over the Church of Rome,' and 'Popery calmly considered.' *Works*, Vol. X.

unkind thoughts for these are the root of bitterness. Lastly, they were to endeavour to help each other in whatever helped forward the Kingdom of God. They were always to be glad to strengthen each other's hands in God. He signed the letter—Your affectionate servant.

His private dealings with Roman Catholics were always friendly. He declared in his pamphlet, *A disavowal of persecuting Papists*, that he knew of many Catholics who sincerely loved both God and their neighbour, and endeavoured to do unto every one as they would wish him to do to them. He had a verbal duel with Father O'Leary, an Irish priest, of nimble wit and great skill in controversy. The six letters of O'Leary addressed to the 'conductors of the free press' in answer to Wesley's *Defence of the Protestant Association* showed him a foeman worthy of Wesley's steel.[1] Indeed it was Boswell's opinion that 'the Capuchin gave Wesley a drubbing.'[2] It was this very priest who had proved so formidable in debate that Wesley sought out seven years later. He had breakfast with him and enjoyed the visit greatly. He found O'Leary to be of 'easy genteel carriage and not wanting either in sense or learning.'[3] There was another direction in which Wesley showed his tolerance of Roman Catholicism. He recommended certain Catholic books of devotion and of learning to his people. Included in the list of his published works for the use of Methodists was *A treatise on the Imitation of Christ*. Written in Latin by Thomas à Kempis. Abridged and published in England by the Rev. John Wesley: *The Life of Gregory Lopez*: written originally in Spanish; abridged by the Rev. John Wesley, A.M.: *An extract of the Life of Madame Guyon*, by John Wesley, A.M. 1776: *Desiderii Erasmi Colloquia selecta. In Usum juventutis Christianae*, 1750. This list, short as it is, shows his acquaintance with phases of Catholic literature and his willingness to use it for his people.

Despite his wide tolerance and his regard for the devotional literature of Catholicism, Wesley had a deep mistrust of every Roman Catholic. His letter to the *London Chronicle* in 1761 had three main contentions. He said the Church of Rome was not founded by Christ, neither was it a unity nor was it holy. He

---

[1] See also A. O'Leary, *Humane Remonstrance to Scottish and English Inquisitors*.
[2] *Journal*, Vol. VII, p. 274 n.
[3] *ibid.*, May 12, 1787, Vol. VII, p. 274.

declared that the generality of its members were no more holy than Turks or heathens. 'You need not go far for proof of this. Look at Romanists in London or in Dublin, just such holiness is the bottomless pit.'[1]

His main contention against the Church of Rome was its untrustworthiness. He said a Roman Catholic Council had decreed that no faith was to be kept with heretics. Since a Romanist acknowledged the absolute authority of the Pope, he was not able to render full allegiance to a temporal monarch. The Pope could pardon treason and rebellion as well as every other sin. These views Wesley expressed repeatedly. There is no doubt that he regarded Catholics as potential enemies of the King.[2] In this one particular he was intolerant. He was perfectly willing to tolerate their religious views, even though he differed so radically, but he could not tolerate the heresy of their political opinions. He believed that if Catholics were granted any measure of freedom they would prove a danger to the State.

By an Act of 1700 priests could be punished by imprisonment. The estates of Romanists living abroad were forfeited in favour of Protestant heirs. Roman Catholics were not allowed to acquire real property except by descent. These repressive measures were repealed by the Saville Act of 1778, but no attempt was made in that Act to secure full freedom of worship and action for Roman Catholics. They were still debarred from the universities and from public offices. It was only a very mild measure of reform. Wesley, however, declared that the Roman faith was rapidly increasing. Through the liberty afforded by the Saville Act, it was preached without let or hindrance. Chapels were built and schools were opened. Wesley wrote to *Freeman's Journal* pleading that the Act of 1700 be reinforced. Though he lent his support to the intolerant Protestant Association, it was the support of his heart rather than his head. He never liked the methods adopted by the Association, nor did he believe in their efficacy. He had a certain regard for Lord George Gordon, but distrusted his leadership of the movement. The Gordon Riots he greatly deplored. It is to the credit of Methodists in London, that when the persecuting zeal of Protestants was at its height and Papists were being hunted down, they

[1] *ibid*., Vol. VII, February 19, 1761.
[2] 'Letter to *Public Advertiser*,' 'Two Letters to *Freeman's Journal*,' 'Letter quoted in *Protestants Magazine*,' 1783.

H

sought out and befriended the fugitives until the danger was passed. During those days the preachers dwelt on the need for peace and charity.

The most serious consequence of Wesley's distrust of Romanists, and his opposition to Roman Catholic Relief, was that he infected his successors with like sentiments. Methodism adopted his views and for half a century at least, a positive hatred was shown towards the Roman Catholic Church. Methodists could not even share his tolerance of their beliefs. The only note his successors sounded was one of warning against Romish practices and Romish influence.

In the years following Wesley's death the *Methodist Magazine* only referred to Roman Catholicism in order to condemn it. Its attitude to Roman Catholic emancipation was clear and uncompromising. In its pages was quoted, with benign approval, a writer who claimed that Roman Catholic emancipation would be a most dangerous encroachment on Church and State, and that it would be highly impolitic to trust to such an extent people who are manifestly prone to rebellion.[1]

In the same year the *Magazine* published an article 'On Popery' which expressed similar sentiments, with the same belief in the perfidy of Catholics.

Joseph Butterworth may be taken as representing the most enlightened and tolerant Methodist point of view. At a meeting convened in the library, Redcross Street, on April 30, 1812, representatives of three religious denominations were assembled to seek the repeal of penal statutes in religious worship. The meeting agreed to forward a petition to Parliament pleading for complete liberty in religious worship. Joseph Butterworth was at that time Member of Parliament for Coventry, and when the petition was presented before the House of Commons, he rose and declared that the meeting which had forwarded the petition was not unanimous. This aroused much indignation on the part of those who had attended the meeting, because Butterworth had not been present. His information was therefore not at first hand, nor was it strictly accurate. One of the conveners declared that there was virtual unanimity, and that the sole purpose of Butterworth's speech was to weaken the force of the petition in the estimation of the Commons.[2]

[1] *Methodist Magazine*, March 1812.
[2] J. Evans, *Complete Religious Liberty Vindicated*, 1813.

The reason was guessed at once and indeed it is the only possible explanation. Butterworth was afraid that the people to benefit most from such a petition were Roman Catholics. He was strenuously opposed to any form of relief for them and therefore he minimized the importance of the petition which had been presented. Richard Carlile wrote sneeringly in his periodical 'How perfectly consistent for Butterworth and Wilberforce to refuse all concessions to Roman Catholics.'[1]

Methodist Ministers shared the views of Butterworth, and Jabez Bunting expressed repeatedly his abhorrence of the Church of Rome.[2]

The influence of Methodism was partly instrumental in the defeat of Grattan's Bill which was a moderate measure seeking to make Romanists eligible for Parliament and public offices. It was debated four days in the Commons in May 1813, and was finally rejected by 251 to 247, a narrow majority of four.[3]

The consequence of this attitude was that in the agitation for Roman Catholic emancipation, Methodists were most powerful in opposition. Daniel O'Connell was in the curious position of having to applaud them as the most active workers of the abolition of slavery, and to condemn them as the most bitter opponents of Roman Catholic Relief.[4] As late as January 1846 *The Watchman*, a Methodist paper of high repute, spoke of the Roman Church as an 'idolatrous, superstitious, treacherous and tyrannical system.'

It is a matter for regret that Wesley's tolerance was imperfect, and that he bequeathed to his followers an unfortunate legacy. It is even more to be lamented that his followers showed no tolerance, and conducted their opposition with fierce hostility. However, a partial defence can be made. Methodism of the early nineteenth century had the excuse of only sharing a common catch cry. 'No Popery' was an ever-popular slogan. The last fight for freedom in religion, as in other spheres, had hardly yet begun. It was to come with Benthamite legislation and be the crowning achievement of a utilitarian philosophy.

[1] *The Republican*, September 12, 1823, Vol. VIII, p. 290.
[2] Cf. *The Watchman*, January 7, 1846.
[3] See *Protestant Advocate*, 1813–1816.
[4] *Whig Radicalism against Wesleyan Methodism*, 1841. Also *Anti-Slavery Monthly Reporter*, Vol. IV, p. 271, 1831.

CHAPTER IV

HUMANITARIANISM

THOUGH Wesley was a Tory in politics he was essentially liberal in his attitude to the poor and sick and unprivileged. This was quite consistent with his thorough-going Toryism. It was Tory philanthropists such as Shaftesbury, Sadler and Oastler who fought for the Factory Acts, and Radicals like Bright who bitterly opposed them. One reason was that Radicals were so often manufacturers and therefore unable to judge impartially the case for factory legislation. The whole record of the nineteenth-century social legislation shows that Radicals had no monopoly in humanitarian reform.

Wesley derived his humanitarianism directly from the Bible. The injunction of Jesus to visit the prisons, care for the sick, clothe the naked, feed the hungry, he accepted as part of that conduct which issues from faith. He believed social welfare to be the responsibility of the individual and not the State. It was the duty and privilege of the rich to help the poor, of the learned to enlighten the ignorant, of the saint to seek the sinner. He placed his whole reliance on individual endeavour.

Wesley was one of the first to discover the poor. The prevailing Poor Law suggested the national attitude. Poverty was a stigma. If men were unable to provide for themselves, they must be helped, but the duty never became a pleasure. Religious bodies had only accomplished a small amount of good. The Church had inspired societies with charitable aims but it had not directly encouraged their growth. Such societies were small, and the work they did was confined to the Metropolis. The Society for the Reformation of Manners, which began in the last decade of the seventeenth century, must not be confused with the religious societies which began at the same time. It was austere in outlook as its title suggests. Offenders against social morality were sought out assiduously and punished, but it did no constructive work. Wilberforce revived the Society at the end of the eighteenth century but its character remained the same.

HUMANITARIANISM

John Wesley helped to make England conscious of its social obligations. He gave Methodism a foremost place among the Churches in works of benevolence and charity. Throughout the nineteenth century Methodism bore an honourable name for philanthropic enterprise. There was one particular direction in which the work Wesley did for the poor was continued by his successors. Towards the end of his life in 1787 he started Benevolent or Strangers' Friend Societies. They were thrown open to the poor of all Churches and quickly established themselves as agencies of relief. Many thousands from all denominations benefited.

Wesley recorded in his *Journal* for March 14, 1790, that he met the Strangers' Friend Society in Bristol 'instituted wholly for the relief not of our Society but for poor, sick, friendless strangers.' He said he had never heard of such an institution till a few years ago and that it must be reckoned one of the fruits of Methodism. One of his last letters was written to Adam Clarke (February 9, 1791). He congratulated him on setting up the Strangers' Friend Society and spoke of it as an excellent institution.

In an old history of Liverpool, there is an interesting reference to the Strangers' Friend Society: 'This Society originated among the Methodists of the town and is in great measure supported by them. The principles upon which it rests are liberal in the extreme and reflect the greatest honour on the sect. It included the wretched of every religious persuasion except their own, who are relieved from another fund. The only recommendation is distress.'[1]

The fund for the relief of the Methodist poor mentioned in the article was known as the Poor Fund. It was usually collected from offerings at the Sacrament of the Lord's Supper, and from grants given from the general fund of the Church. The conference of 1805 spoke of the great increase of charitable institutions among Wesleyans. The Address mentioned, in particular, Sunday Schools for the education of poor children, and benevolent Societies for the relief of the sick and poor of all denominations. It praised the liberal manner in which Methodists were supporting these institutions.

Wesley began in 1746 to give medicine to the poor. In six months hundreds of cases had been treated. He then opened a dispensary at Bristol which in a short time had dealt with two hundred people. In London he established four centres, where patients could receive electric treatment, and Wesley claimed that great numbers

[1] J. Smith, *History of Liverpool*, 1810.

were benefited.[1] He also started a 'lending stock' to assist poor Methodists at the Foundry. Any poor person could obtain a loan of £1 to £5 on the recommendation of a class leader if someone became security for repayment. When the idea took shape in 1746, the capital amounted to £30 and from it over two hundred were helped in eighteen months. Later Wesley made a special appeal and the capital rose to £120. Stewards attended weekly to distribute the loans, and money was paid back within three months by weekly instalments.

These schemes do not appear to have survived Wesley's death. There is no mention of them in nineteenth-century Methodism though it is possible that the 'lending stock' still existed within the Metropolis itself. The charitable work of early nineteeth-century Methodism was confined largely to the visitation of prisons and institutions, and to the relief of distress.

There were certain social evils against which Wesley entered an emphatic and effective protest. His protest against drinking and gambling, though sustained by his followers after his death, made slight difference to the habits of his countrymen, but in his crusade against the plundering of wrecked vessels and smuggling, his successors continuing his work saw a real abatement of the evils.

There is no more splendid page in Methodist history than the transformation of Cornwall. The people were addicted to the practice of plundering vessels which had been wrecked upon the rocks of their coast. Sometimes there was a deliberate attempt to decoy the vessels to their doom. Wesley found in 1776 that the practice still continued save that no Methodist would have anything to do with it. He suggested that the gentry of Cornwall might stamp it out by refusing to employ the offenders.[2] The preachers who ministered in Cornwall after his death, continued to preach against it, and in the first quarter of the nineteenth century the practice almost died out.

Smuggling was another evil which Wesley would not tolerate in his Society. If a rumour spread which concerned the culpability of any member he made the most patient and searching investigations. If the rumour was based on truth, the guilty person was immediately expelled. He wrote a powerful pamphlet entitled

---

[1] L. Tyerman, *Life and Times of John Wesley*, Vol. I, p. 525. A. Stevens, *History of Methodism*, Vol. I, p. 371.

[2] *Journal*, August 17, 1775.

HUMANITARIANISM

Word to a Smuggler in 1767. In the pamphlet he defined many kinds of smuggling and condemned them on two grounds. First he said it was robbing the king: robbing a good father who loved and tried to help his subjects; then it was robbing one's fellows, for losses on duties meant increased taxation. In the last section Wesley considered the various excuses made for the practice and showed how unsatisfactory they were. The pamphlet finished with a plea for uprightness and honesty.

The pamphlet was circulated long after Wesley's death and the preachers also continued to enforce his prohibition. The Conference of 1806 raised the whole issue and urged that since smuggling though much decreased still continued to exist, it was the duty of every Methodist to use his influence to stamp out the practice. The Conference recommended that the *Word to a Smuggler* should be carefully dispersed; that all who would not renounce smuggling should be expelled and that every local preacher who attempted to defend it should be silenced. As a consequence of Methodist propaganda, smuggling was materially reduced, though even to-day the smuggler is not a romantic figure of the past.

Humanitarianism in the early nineteenth century is connected with the Evangelical Revival in the Church. Through the efforts of Evangelicals came many reforms in prison conditions and in the penal code. Together with Benthamites they helped to secure the abolition of the whipping of women (1820): the partial abolition of the pillory: the protection of animals (1822): the abolition of State lotteries (1820-1827) and the prohibition of spring guns (1827). From the same impulse came enactments for the protection of children, such as forbidding their employment as chimney sweeps.[1] The Health and Morals Act of 1802 was an example of Evangelical influence in legislation. It was introduced by the father of Sir Robert Peel and was intended to regulate the employment of apprentices in cotton and woollen factories. Among the rules for sanitation and right living, was the injunction that 'every apprentice should on Sunday for the space of an hour be instructed and examined in the principles of the Christian religion by a qualified person.'[2] The Act was never thoroughly enforced, but it did at least express the sentiments of good Evangelical Churchmen.

There was no determined and agreed alliance between Metho-

[1] A. V. Dicey, *Law and Opinion in England*, pp. 106 and 189.
[2] *ibid.*, p. 110.

dists and Evangelicals in humanitarian reform. Even in Wesley's own day the precursors of the Evangelical Revival in the Church were not allied to Wesley save in sympathy and friendliness. They gave him the freedom of their parishes and the benefit of their hospitality, but they were in no way associated with the development of his work.

It is perhaps necessary to distinguish between the clergymen who were his friends and sympathetic to his work. Wesley himself told Dr. Byrom that he divided his assistants into regulars, half-regulars, and irregulars.[1] His Anglican friends can broadly be placed in two classes. Walker of Truro, Henry Venn, Berridge of Everton, and Romaine associated for many years with St. Dunstan's Church, London, were Evangelical clergymen who were indefatigable in their desire to save souls. They were Wesley's friends and correspondents but they did not actively associate themselves with the development of his work.

On the other hand, Grimshaw of Haworth definitely lent his assistance to Wesley from 1748 till his death in 1762. He took charge of two large Methodist Circuits in addition to his own work, and he conducted class meetings and love feasts and preaching services with untiring zeal. The travelling preachers were always welcomed at Haworth. They were sure of generous hospitality. When need arose he was willing to give up his bed and sleep in the barn in order to provide extra accommodation. Vincent Perronet, the vicar of Shoreham, was for many years the counsellor and friend of John Wesley and his brother. Two of his sons became Methodist preachers and Charles Perronet especially was a leader in Methodist enterprise. The greatest name of all is that of Fletcher, who refused a comfortable parish with a large income, and became vicar of Madeley in Shropshire, which was at that time a rough mining community. When he was asked if any preferment would be acceptable to him, he said, 'I want nothing but more grace.' From 1757 until his death in 1785 he was the most trusted and valuable ally that Wesley possessed. He was not only an earnest and successful preacher, but a scholar of no mean attainment. He served the cause of religion greatly by his pen. The fresh outbreak of the Calvinistic controversy in 1777 provoked his *Checks to Antinomianism*, which was the finest theological work the unhappy dispute produced. His labours among the Methodist Societies,

[1] *Journal*, Vol. II, p. 629.

and his part in the annual Conferences, marked him out as the natural successor to John Wesley. When he died, Wesley said of him, 'I have known many excellent men, holy in heart and life, but one equal to him I have not known, one so uniformly and deeply devoted to God.'[1]

There were some devoted preachers in the Methodist Church who had been episcopally ordained, chief among them was Dr. Coke who in 1777 threw in his lot with Methodism. Others are known only because of their association with Wesley's chapel and the work in London. Such were James Creighton and Peard Dickinson.

As Methodism gradually became separated from the Church so the co-operation between Methodists and Evangelicals became less close and intimate. Those who had remained outside Methodism and pursued their work within their parish boundaries, encouraged the growth of Evangelicalism within the Established Church. When Romaine began to preach there were only six or seven clergymen with Evangelical views, but when he died in 1795 there were more than 500.[2]

The decision of Wesley in 1784 to ordain Coke as superintendent for the work in America, with instructions to ordain Asbury as a co-superintendent, came as a grievous shock to Anglican sentiment. Once his mind was resolved, however, he did not hesitate to ordain others to the work in America, Scotland, and even in England itself. Lord Mansfield had declared that ordination was separation, and many of Wesley's close friends were in agreement. His own brother, Charles, wrote more than one letter of entreaty and reproach. The letter failed to move John for the step he took was no hasty decision. As early as 1746 Lord King's book, *Account of the Primitive Church*, had convinced him that apostolic succession was a fable 'which no man ever did or ever can prove.' He wrote to Charles that he firmly believed himself to be as much a scriptural επισκοπος as any man in England or Europe. Charles on his side relieved his feelings by the famous epigram:

> How easily are Bishops made
> By man or woman's whim.
> Wesley his hand on Coke hath laid
> But who laid hands on him?

---

[1] *Works*, Vol. XI, p. 365.
[2] *Life of Henry Venn*, p. 14. (Quoted by Telford, *John Wesley*, p. 313.)

The love which the two men had for each other was too strong to be broken even by so serious a divergence of views. John pleaded for his brother's continued friendship and Charles replied: 'I thank you for your intention to remain my friend. Here is my heart as your heart. Whom God hath joined let no man put asunder. We have taken each other for better for worse, till death us do part, but to unite eternally.' There were others beside Charles who refused to let the ordinations disturb their friendship with John, but necessarily the action was the first widening of the breach between Methodism and the Established Church.

In 1787 John Wesley was forced to register his chapels as Dissenting places of worship, in order to license them, and avoid the fines levied through the Conventicle Act. Continued agitation throughout Methodism caused him in 1788 to allow Methodist services where necessary to be held in Church hours. In 1795 Methodist ministers were allowed to administer the Sacrament of the Lord's Supper. All these steps widened the distance between Methodists and the Evangelicals. The death of Wesley in 1791 was in itself a grievous blow to any close agreement and co-operation. His name was revered by Methodists and Evangelicals alike. There were doctrinal differences that even in Wesley's day had caused some pain and now assumed more importance. Methodists were Arminians, whilst Evangelicals were moderate Calvinists. None of the outstanding personalities of the Evangelical revival showed any particular interest in Methodism except Wilberforce, and none identified himself with any of its activities. On the contrary Hannah More, who may fairly be taken as a typical Evangelical of the early nineteenth century, said she had employed a Mrs. Easterbrook as a mistress of a Sunday School but she confessed, 'I am afraid she is a Methodist.'[1] On another occasion a clergyman dismissed a teacher for being a Methodist, with her full concurrence.[2] She spoke in high terms of a Sergeant Hill, 'whom we thought at first to be a Methodist, but we find him so good a soldier, and so correct in his morals, that we do not trouble ourselves about his religion.'[3] This would suggest that no sort of alliance existed between the Evangelicals and Methodists.

There were two main centres of the Evangelical Revival. One was at Cambridge, where Simeon collected around him a body of

[1] Annette Meakin, *Life of Hannah More*, p. 293.
[2] *ibid.*, p. 329.　　　[3] *ibid.*, p. 332.

staunch Evangelicals. The other was at Clapham, where clergy and laity met regularly for prayer and discussions and the promotion of charitable schemes. The remarkable feature of the Clapham Sect was that laymen were so prominent and their influence so great. The meetings were attended by Joseph Butterworth, who was a well-known Methodist and philanthropist. In turn, leading Evangelicals such as Teignmouth, Wilberforce, and Zachary Macaulay discussed their philanthropic schemes at the town residence of Butterworth in Fleet Street. It was at his house that the first meetings of the British and Foreign Bible Society were held. Joseph Butterworth was Member of Parliament for Coventry between 1812 and 1818, and for Dover between 1820 and 1826. Throughout his career he maintained his friendly relations with Evangelicals, and identified himself with them in their humanitarian reforms.

Thomas Thompson was an equally prominent Methodist Member of parliament and philanthropist. He was a friend of the Evangelical leaders, and was a welcome and constant attender at Clapham. He was not one whit behind Butterworth in his philanthropy and his support of humanitarian reform. There were other Methodists such as Adam Clarke, and Dr. Coke who had been ordained in the Church before he entered the Methodist ministry. They were on terms of friendship with Evangelicals and more especially with the leading laymen of the movement. The position, therefore, was that the two bodies did not work together nor seek any common understanding, but certain leaders on each side were friends and acted co-operatively in philanthropic schemes.

Since Methodists and Evangelicals were both distinguished for their good works, it is inevitable that without any conscious planning, they should find themselves working for a common end in great humanitarian enterprises. An outstanding example is the way in which both worked for the abolition of slavery. But though their mind was one on great social issues, their action was often independent. The ties that bound them were not close and formal, but were formed out of the personal and friendly relations of prominent men on each side. That such a relationship should exist is sufficiently intelligible when one realizes that both Methodism and the Evangelical movement were born out of the same revival of religion: both had the same views of the manners and habits of their countrymen, and both sought to show their faith in personal conduct and in humanitarian reform.

PART IV
METHODISM AND THE SOCIAL LIFE OF THE DAY

CHAPTER I

METHODISM AND THE SOCIAL LIFE OF THE DAY

METHODISTS defined rigidly the things that belonged to the world and the things that belonged to God. They felt they had been called out of an evil world into the new life of the Spirit. The services on the Sunday and the class meetings in the week occupied their leisure hours. They looked with suspicion on all amusements and recreations.

The theatre was regarded with special distrust. John Wesley himself had opposed with great determination the opening of a new playhouse in Bristol. He wrote to the Mayor and Corporation protesting strongly against the proposal.[1] He called the English theatre 'the sink of all profaneness and debauchery,'[2] and when in his *Manners of the Present Times* he affirmed lewdness was not yet universal, he qualified that by saying, 'we are making swift advances towards it through playhouses, masquerades, and pantheons.' The prejudice of John Wesley against the theatre was fully shared by his successors. The *Methodist Magazine* in 1814 contained an article which dwelt at length on the evil of contemporary amusements, and more especially on the menace and danger of the theatre. When the *Quarterly Review* made its scathing condemnation of the moroseness of Methodism, one of the main charges in the indictment was the violent antipathy of Methodists to the theatre. The reviewer said that when Covent Garden and Drury Lane were destroyed, it was the occasion of rejoicing and thanksgiving among many Methodists.[3] The *Edinburgh Review* made a similar charge, and lashed Methodists for their opposition to theatres and to other fashionable amusements.[4] It was not merely that Methodists would not go to theatres; in his *Advice to the People called Methodists* John Wesley said that Methodists would doubtless be blamed for refusing even to read plays.[5]

[1] December 20, 1764.
[2] *Works*, Vol. VII, p. 34.
[3] *Quarterly Review*, November 1810, Vol. IV, p. 491.
[4] *Edinburgh Review*, January 1808.
[5] *Works*, Vol. VIII, p. 354.

Methodists were equally severe on dancing, on snuff-taking and on smoking, and condemned them in Conference and in the Connexional Magazine.[1] Wesley declared that balls and public dancing made debauchery easy unless practised with the same caution as among the heathen, where men and women never danced together but always in separate rooms.[2] In one of his letters to Miss Bishop he said that though dancing might not be evil in itself, it might lead young women to numberless evils and therefore was to be avoided.[3] This again was one of the points of criticism made in the *Quarterly* and in the *Edinburgh Reviews*.

A more serious feature of the dissociation of the Methodists from the world in which they lived, was the neglect of literature and music. Wesley published one novel among the books he issued during his lifetime. It was Henry Brooke's *Fool of Quality*. This was very displeasing to many of the preachers who expressed their disapprobation. John Easton was one of these. After John had very freely criticized the conduct of Wesley in publishing such a book, Wesley met him and spoke to him of some of the characters in the book.

Wesley: 'Did you read Vindez, John?'
Easton: 'Yes, sir.'
W.: 'Did you laugh, John?'
E.: 'No, sir.'
W.: 'Did you read Damon and Pythias, John?'
E.: 'Yes, sir.'
W.: 'Did you cry, John?'
E.: 'No, sir.'
W. lifting up his eyes, and clasping his hands, exclaimed: 'O earth—earth—earth!'[4]

But even Wesley stated without comment that Methodists neither 'read romances nor books of humour nor talked in a merry, gay, diverting manner.'[5] One of the foremost leaders in the generation which succeeded Wesley was John Pawson, who became President of the Conference on two occasions (1798 and 1811).

[1] *Methodist Magazine*, 1814.
[2] *Works*, Vol. VII, p. 34.
[3] *ibid.*, Vol. XIII, p. 39.
[4] Rev. L. Tyerman, *Life and Times of Wesley*, Vol. III, p. 342. cf. Everett's *Life of Clarke*.
[5] 'Advice to people called Methodists.' *Works*, Vol. VIII, p. 354.

He had received a better education than most of Wesley's preachers, and yet he burnt Wesley's annotated edition of Shakespeare's Works as 'useless lumber.'[1] The *Arminian*, and later the *Methodist Magazine*, was occupied exclusively with sermons, articles on matters of faith, remarkable visitations of Providence, letters and memoirs of devout Methodists. A criticism of its narrow scope had been made even before Wesley died and Wesley had replied that it was a Magazine designed to state the doctrine of universal redemption and had no other pretensions.[2] The fact remains that this was the only periodical the Society possessed for many years.

Quite apart from the narrow range of the Magazine, the Methodist Book-Room in the years following Wesley's death published almost entirely religious works or works connected with religion. Methodist authors in the early nineteenth century devoted themselves either to publishing sermons or to writing memoirs. The more learned, such as Coke, Clarke, Benson and Sutcliffe, published Commentaries on the Bible or wrote philosophical treatises. The sketches of lives and deaths of devout Christians were plentiful, and were eagerly read. There was indeed a great reading public for religious works. One of the chief means of propaganda used by Evangelicals was the pamphlet. The early nineteenth century was the golden age of the religious pamphlet. Thousands of copies were sold and the mode of writing only gradually came into disrepute. The satire of Dickens and Wilkie Collins marked the final decline of its popularity.

In the early years of the nineteenth century, religious books were best sellers. A Bedfordshire clergyman, named Legh Richmond, wrote a simple story with a strongly religious flavour. It was called *The Dairyman's Daughter*, and it had a sale of two million copies. Remembering the relatively small population of England, this is an enormous figure. Perhaps nothing is more significant than the way in which the works of Hannah More were read by thousands of people. Other books were only less popular. Such solid works as Paley's *Evidences of Christianity*, Hervey's *Meditations*, Young's *Night Thoughts*, Dean Milman's *Ecclesiastical History* and above all William Wilberforce's *Practical View of the Prevailing Religious Systems contrasted with Real Christianity*, reached a very large public. Books such as Milton's Poems, especially his *Paradise*

[1] *New History of Methodism*, Vol. I, p. 389.
[2] *Works*, Vol. XIV, p. 363.

Lost, and Bunyan's *Pilgrim's Progress* were in every educated household.[1] Methodists shared in this supply of religious literature. They produced no playwright, no novelist, no historian, not even a social and political pamphleteer as Wesley in his versatility had been. But they did produce men who wrote religious pamphlets and biographies.[2] One of the criticisms against Methodism was the narrowness of its range of literature.[3] This was not only true of the writers but of the readers. When John Wesley wrote to Walter Churchey (August 8, 1788) he said, 'Methodists do not care to buy or even read (at least the generality) anything but religious books.' Thomas Jackson said in 1839, the year of his Presidency, that Methodists had no time for light literature. They read chiefly the Methodist Hymn Book and the Bible.[4]

Music was conceived in the same narrow terms. Wesley had commented on the fact that in Methodism there was no singing of innocent songs,[5] but he was at least fond of music. He published five musical works. His *Sacred Harmony* was designated as a choice collection of psalms and hymn tunes in two or three parts, for the voice, harpsichord and organ. This was revised and issued at three separate periods in his life.[6]

Wesley had no time for anthems because he believed wholeheartedly in congregational singing. His directions for congregational singing are still pertinent and valuable.[7] His views were held by his successors. Indeed they interpreted more narrowly the scope of music. The Conference of 1805 laid down the rule that no musical festivals or selections of sacred music be encouraged or permitted in our chapels.[8] The twentieth question of the Conference had reference to singing. The answer was, that no instrument of music be introduced into the singers' seats except the bass viol. No pieces in which recitatives were sung by single men, solos by single women, fuguing (or different words sung by different

---

[1] On this whole subject of reading see Amy Cruse, *The Englishman and his Books in the Nineteenth Century*.
[2] cf. The Bibliography.
[3] *Quarterly Review*, November 1810.
[4] *Centenary of Wesleyan Methodism*, 1839.
[5] 'Advice to Methodists,' *Works*, Vol. VIII, p. 354.
[6] See 'Musical Works published by the Rev. John Wesley,' *Works*, Vol. XIV, p. 345.
[7] *Works*, Vol. XIV, p. 345. See Appendix II.
[8] Quoted by *Evangelical Magazine*, Vol. XIII, p. 524.

METHODISM AND THE SOCIAL LIFE OF THE DAY 131

voices at the same time) were to be permitted.[1] In the next year Conference placed a ban on organs.[2] They held the view that organ and special music introduced an alien note into a Methodist service. They desired the whole burden of singing to be borne by the congregation alone. In 1813 the Wesleyan Conference further defined its views on music when it passed a ban on the singing of 'vain songs.'

Methodists were critical of the manners and habits of their age. They were particularly vehement in their denunciation of spirituous liquors. In 1689 the importation of foreign spirits was virtually prohibited and distillation on the payment of certain duties was thrown open to all Englishmen. This helped to make the drinking of alcohol a national habit. In 1694, 527,000 gallons of spirits had been distilled, but by 1750 the number had risen to 11,000,000 gallons.[3] The Government became aware of the growing evil, and between 1736 and 1753 three Acts were passed which imposed duties on liquor, restricted the freedom of distillers, and limited the number of public houses.[4] Unfortunately these Acts made no practical difference. The trade continued to flourish and increase.

John Wesley was one of the first to see danger in the sale of alcohol and to denounce the trade in alcohol publicly.

'We may not sell our neighbour anything which tends to impair health. Such is, eminently, all that liquid fire, commonly called drams, or spirituous liquors. It is true, these may have a place in medicine; they may be of use in some bodily disorders; although there would rarely be occasion for them, were it not for the unskilfulness of the practitioner. Therefore, such as prepare and sell them only for this end may keep their conscience clear. But who are they? Who prepare them only for this end? Do you know ten such distillers in England? Then excuse these. But all who sell them in the common way, to any that will buy, are poisoners general. They murder His Majesty's subjects by wholesale, neither does their eye pity or spare. They drive them to hell like sheep. And what is their gain? Is it not the blood of these men? Who then would envy their large estates and sumptuous palaces? A curse is in the midst of them: the curse of God cleaves to the stones, the timber, the furniture of them! The curse of God is in their gardens, their walks, their groves; a fire that burns to the nethermost hell! Blood, blood is there: the foundations, the floor, the walls, the roof, are stained with blood! And canst thou hope, O thou man of blood,

---

[1] *Minutes of Conference*, 1805.
[2] *Evangelical Magazine*, Vol. XVI, p. 489.
[3] J. S. Simon, *Revival of England in the Eighteenth Century*, pp. 88-90.
[4] *ibid.*, pp. 91-92.

though thou art "clothed in scarlet and fine linen, and farest sumptuously every day"; canst thou hope to deliver down thy fields of blood to the third generation? Not so; for there is a God in heaven. Therefore, thy name shall soon be rooted out. Like as those whom thou hast destroyed, body and soul, "thy memorial shall perish with thee".'[1]

In his *Thoughts on Nervous Disorders*, Wesley once more inveighed against the traffic in drink. He declared himself astonished that the preparing and selling of the poison should be permitted in any civilized country. To the objection that it brought revenue to the Government, he answered that it was blood money.[2] In another pamphlet he argued that food was dear because of the immense quantities of corn consumed in this way in distilling, and he stoutly maintained that since spirituous liquors were a deadly poison, destroying not only the strength but the morals of Englishmen, it was imperative for distilling to be abolished.[3]

Those who became Methodists undertook to taste no spirituous liquors and no drams of any kind unless prescribed by a physician.[4] Preachers were not allowed to take drams on any account.[5] To his countrymen in general Wesley pleaded in no measured language: 'You see the wine when it sparkles in the cup, and are going to drink of it. I tell you there is poison in it and I beg you to throw it away.'[6]

Methodists who succeeded Wesley, followed his example, and Methodism continued to enforce the injunction against any use of spirituous liquors. The stricter Methodists went even further and refused to drink tea. This also was in the tradition of Wesley; he drank tea, but only infrequently, and then weak and in small quantities. The injunction of Wesley was not directed against all liquors. Wesley wondered why people should drink tea when they could drink instead, good home-brewed English ale. Within two generations of his death, it was a regular custom to drink home-brewed beer at Circuit dinners and Sunday School festivals.[7] The vigour of Wesley's protest against the trade in alcohol was not sustained so strongly after his death. Gradually Methodism lost the

[1] *Works*, Vol. VI, pp. 128-129.
[2] *ibid.*, Vol. XI, p. 516.
[3] *Thoughts on the present Scarcity of Provisions*, 1773.
[4] *Directions to Band Societies*, December 25, 1744.
[5] *Works*, Vol. VIII, p. 307.
[6] Sermon 'On Public Diversions.' *Works*, Vol. VII, p. 504.
[7] *New History of Methodism*, Vol. I, p. 329.

lead in the denunciation of the traffic. It is true that the Conference of 1836 bewailed the sin of intemperance, but in 1841 Wesleyan chapels were forbidden to allow their premises to be used for teetotal meetings. When a Temperance declaration was drawn up in 1848 it had the signature of only forty-eight Wesleyan ministers. It was not until 1873, when a Committee was set up to promote Temperance legislation, that the work of Wesley was continued with vigour. Under the leadership of Charles Garrett, T. Bowman Stephenson and Hugh Price Hughes the Temperance movement in Methodism made rapid progress.

In the generation after Wesley, Methodists, though loyal to Wesley's denunciation of spirits, did not by speech or pen continue his crusade against distilling. His words were allowed to fall to the ground. His successors did not dream of using legislative methods, and mere protest seemed so hopeless. They relied more on the force of example than the use of argument.

Methodists were not only opposed to spirituous liquors, but to gambling. The gambling habit was so deep-rooted in England that the *European Magazine* made the suicide of a young gambler the opportunity of denouncing a mania which had infected the nation.[1] The *Anti-Jacobin Review* described the progress of gambling as so alarming that it was as much practised in the private parties of tradesmen as in the public room of clubs.[2] Piggott in his *Political Dictionary* said that gambling originated in avarice, was universally predominant, and raged through all ranks and conditions of Society. Wesley deplored the laying of wagers because he declared it fostered covetousness, and led to a lust for money which no winnings could wholly satisfy. He said no sport could justify itself which corrupted even one person through the gambling associated with it.[3] He denounced sharpers and gamesters as public nuisances and scandals to the English nation.[4] Incidentally it is interesting to note that he was not violently opposed to Lotteries. He said in a letter to David Gordon, October 19, 1787, that he himself had never bought a lottery ticket but he did not blame those who had.

Wesley attacked horse racing because it filled the mind with love of pleasure more than love of God. He believed it made men

[1] *European Magazine*, January 1782, p. 74.
[2] *Anti-Jacobin Review*, Vol. VII, p. 274, also 1800, p. 141.
[3] Sermon 'On Public Diversions.' *Works*, Vol. VII, p. 505.
[4] *Works*, Vol. VIII, p. 164.

spend on an idle sport what their wives and families needed at home. Even if no money was spent, said Wesley, it was a waste of that time which might have been spent in honest labour.[1] So hotly did his successors dislike gambling that even card games were forbidden.[2] They were regarded as games spoilt by the gambling habit.

It is surprising that Methodists did not even refer to, much less attack, the sports and pastimes of the day. The reason, as given by Wesley himself, was that Methodists had no need specifically to indict them. They stood self-condemned, and those who knew Methodists would also know their attitude to all such sports. Wesley declared that not only among Methodists, but in general Society, many diversions had fallen into great disrepute. He declared that the gentry of England disregarded the once noble art of hawking, just as the common people were no longer amused by men hacking and hewing each other in pieces at broadsword. The game of quarter staff, he said, was only practised by the few, and cudgelling had lost its former glory, even in Wales itself. He declared that public disapprobation was causing bear baiting and bull baiting to disappear. Cock fighting, he believed, was kept alive only because two or three right honourable patrons were interested in it. He called all such pastimes 'foul remains of Gothic barbarity, and a reproach not only to religion but to human nature.'[3] He did not pass so severe a censure on sports of the field. He said that those who had nothing to do could run the foxes and hares out of breath.

The fact that the generation which succeeded Wesley did not refer to the sports of their day, must not therefore be interpreted as acquiescence in them. On the contrary they fully shared Wesley's view and showed by their conduct of life how much they abhorred all such sports.

Wesley was so interested in the question of dress that he preached a sermon on the subject. In his *Journal* and his writings he came back to the matter repeatedly. He believed that costly clothes engendered pride and vanity and other evil passions. He said that money spent unnecessarily on clothes could be better used in the service of poverty and distress. 'See thy expensive apparel: thy gown, thy head-dress! Everything about thee which

---

[1] Sermon 'On Public Diversions.' *Works*, Vol. VII, p. 506.
[2] *Quarterly Review*, November 1810.
[3] Sermon on 'The More Excellent Way.' *Works*, Vol. VII, p. 34.

METHODISM AND THE SOCIAL LIFE OF THE DAY 135

cost more than Christian duty required thee to lay out, is the blood of the poor. Be adorned—with good works.'[1]

He even mentioned specifically the things which displeased him. He said that as people increased in substance their dress became more costly. He bewailed the profusion of ribands, gauze, or linen about the head. Some Methodists had asked him if it was not as sensible to buy fashionable things as unfashionable things. He said, not if they give a bold, immodest appearance, as huge hats, bonnets, and head-dresses always do.[2] In the concluding section of his sermon on Dress, he begged that he might see, before he died, a Methodist congregation dressed as cheaply and plainly as the Quakers. 'Let there be no Quaker Linen—proverbially so called for its exquisite fineness: no Brussels lace, no elephantine hats or bonnets—those scandals of female modesty.'[3]

In his *Advice to Methodists with regard to Dress* Wesley stated most fully the particular objects of dress which he abhorred.

'Wear no gold, no pearls, or precious stones; use no curling of hair, or costly apparel, how grave soever. I advise those who are able to receive this saying, buy no velvets, no silks, no fine linen, no superfluities, no mere ornaments, though ever so much in fashion. Wear nothing, though you have it already, which is of a glaring colour, or which is in any kind gay, glistering, or showy; nothing made in the very height of the fashion, nothing made to attract the eyes of the bystanders. I do not advise women to wear rings, ear-rings, necklaces, lace (of whatever kind or colour), or ruffles, which, little by little, may easily shoot out from one to twelve inches deep. Neither do I advise men to wear coloured waistcoats, shining stockings, glittering or costly buckles or buttons, either on their coats, or in their sleeves, any more than gay, fashionable, or expensive perukes. It is true, these are little, very little things, which are not worth defending, therefore give them up, let them drop, throw them away without another word; else, a little needle may cause much pain in your flesh, a little self-indulgence much hurt to your soul.'[4]

A requirement of membership in the Methodist Church was the avoidance of needless ornaments. In one of the Conference conversations this rule came under discussion.

Q. 16. 'Should we insist on the Band rules particularly with regard to dress?'

A. 'By all means. This is no time to give encouragement to any super-

---

[1] Sermon 'On Dress.' *Works*, Vol. VII, p. 21.
[2] *ibid.*
[3] *ibid.*, p. 24.
[4] *Works*, Vol. XI, p. 469.

fluity of apparel. Therefore give no Band tickets to any till they have left off superfluous ornament. In order to do this, (1) let every Assistant read the "Thought on Dress" at least once a year in every large Society. (2) In visiting the classes be very mild but very strict. (3) Allow no exempt Case not even of a married woman. Better one suffer than many. (4) Give no ticket to any that wear calashes, high-heads, or enormous bonnets.'[1]

After Wesley's death his successors still upheld his injunctions on dress. Those who came into membership were obliged to conform to the rule which proscribed costly dress and needless ornament. Indeed the Conference of 1806 specially declared that the rules regarding dress would be enforced. The Conference set itself the task of bringing to an end 'the unjustifiable custom of men wearing lapelled coats, and expensive and showy stuffs: women wearing short sleeves and long tailed gowns, and children displaying a superfluity of buttons and ribands.'[2]

The last matter in which Methodists were at variance from the customs of the day was in the observance of Sunday. They frowned upon the laxity of its observance and followed the example of Wesley in urging that it be kept wholly sacred. The Conference Address of 1803 dwelt at length upon the Act for raising the army of reserve. They urged any Methodists concerned to avail themselves of the provision whereby people with religious scruples were excused from drill on Sunday and given a time suitable to themselves in the week. It was through the continued protests of Methodists in Jersey, that they were excused from drilling on Sundays. In their appeal (1798) they were warmly supported by Wilberforce.[3] Methodists departed from the accepted custom in refusing to countenance shaving or hair-cutting on a Sunday. It was part of the indictment of the *Quarterly Review* article that Methodists would allow no barbers to work on a Sunday.[4]

This abstention from theatres, dancing, cards, light reading, and singing, snuff-taking and tobacco, and the wearing of fashionable dress, caused people to suspect Methodists of moroseness and melancholy. The chief charge of contemporary criticism was not on the grounds of Methodist doctrine but Methodist practice.

[1] 'Minutes of some late Conversations.' *Works*, Vol. VIII, p. 307.
[2] *Minutes of the Wesleyan Conference*, 1806.
[3] R. I. and S. W. Wilberforce, *Life of William Wilberforce*, Vol. II, p. 315.
[4] *Quarterly Review*, November 1810.

METHODISM AND THE SOCIAL LIFE OF THE DAY 137

Reviewers and writers said that Methodists were confining life to the ambit of chapel and business. Methodists, on their side, deplored the sloth, luxury and indulgence of the age, and deemed their own strictness of conduct necessary. Nor did they condemn all pastimes and recreations. The alternative diversions which Wesley offered to people represented the Methodist point of view. He said that even supposing the reading of plays, novels, and newspapers and the like to be quite innocent, there was a better way. Men of fortune could divert themselves in the open air by cultivating and improving lands; by planting their grounds; by laying out, carrying on, and perfecting gardens and orchards. At other times they could converse with the most serious and sensible of their neighbours. They could visit the sick, poor, widows, and the fatherless, in their affliction. They could read useful history, pious and elegant poetry, and several branches of natural philosophy. If after all this there should be any spare time a person could divert himself by good music or experiments in philosophy.[1]

The influence of Methodism on contemporary Society did not come from protests, however spirited, but by a positive standard of living. When people became Methodists they entered on a way of life which occupied all their leisure hours and left them neither time nor inclination for their former pastimes. It has been rightly said that Methodism took from the pitman 'his dog and fighting cock, and gave him a frock coat for his posy jacket; hymns for his public house ditties, and prayer meetings for his pay-night frolics.'[2] This process was not limited to industrial and mining communities. It was not possible to compromise between the high spiritual standard of life which Methodism demanded and the easy-going indulgent life of contemporary Society. For dissipation was not reckoned merely as frivolity or wrongdoing. It was a life lived without God. In a striking passage Wesley said 'a dissipated life is not barely that of a powdered beau, or a *petit maître*, a gamester, a woman hunter, a playhouse hunter, a fox hunter, or a scatterbrain of any kind; but the life of an honourable statesman, a gentleman, or a merchant that is without God in the world. Agreeably to this a dissipated age (such as is the present beyond all that ever were, at least that are recorded in history) is an age in which God is gener-

[1] *Works*, Vol. VII, p. 35.
[2] E. Welbourne, *The Miners' Union of Northumberland and Durham*, 1923.

ally forgotten. And a dissipated nation (such as England is at present in a superlative degree) is a nation, a vast majority of which have not got God in all their thoughts.'[1]

This challenge to a higher standard of conduct did not at first achieve a startling change. The French Revolution and the war with Napoleon came to unsettle England and retard reform. Yet the revival of religion did leaven Society in a clear and unmistakable manner. Gross brutality in sport disappeared: there came an improvement in the tone of the drama, and J. R. Green was able to speak of the fresh spirit of moral zeal which at the end of the eighteenth century purified our literature and our manners.[2]

[1] *Works*, Vol. VI, p. 448.
[2] J. R. Green, *A Short History of the English People*, p. 718, 1875.

PART V
THE RANGE OF METHODIST INFLUENCE

CHAPTER I

THE NAPOLEONIC PERIOD

IN 1789 there were 56,195 members in the Methodist Church and by 1815 they had risen to 181,709. This number did not include adherents. It meant that in the Napoleonic era 125,514 fresh members had been added. This is a staggering increase for so short a period of time. When other religious bodies had remained practically stationary, Methodism had trebled its membership.

There are certain obvious reasons for this increase. Methodism was able to move with changing England and to seize the opportunities of new areas. The machinery of the Church was more cumbersome and it was not able to adapt itself so easily to new conditions. It had also to contend with private interests which impeded progress. Tithe payers were apprehensive lest an increase of churches would mean an increase in their burdens. Patrons did not view favourably the building of new churches which might reduce the market value of existing livings.[1] The abuses of plurality of livings and of non-residents were notorious. In 1806 the total number of parishes where the incumbent was not resident was stated in Parliament to be 2,423.[2] In view of so many obstacles it is not surprising that even in London only ten new churches were built throughout the whole eighteenth century.[3] Another reason for the increase of Methodism lay in the system of local preaching. This enabled chapels to be built everywhere, even though ministers could only occupy some of the pulpits. The great reason, however, for the success of Methodism lay in the freshness of its message. The theology of Methodism was democratic in its implications. Christian experience was possible to all men. Wesley declared it came not through birth, nor culture, nor intellect, but through a change of heart. Therefore it was free to all. The assertion of universal grace is no longer a live issue, but in Wesley's day it was a real one, and the message of Wesley and his successors was alive and challenging.

[1] E. Halévy, *History of the English People in 1815*, Vol. I, p. 351.
[2] A. F. Freemantle, *England in the Nineteenth Century*, Vol. I, p. 93.
[3] *ibid.*

The increase of members was not evenly distributed. In Scotland, Presbyterianism had too strong a hold over the people for Methodism to make progress. In some of the larger towns there was a Methodist Society, but in no case was it flourishing. In 1790 there were only 1,086 members throughout Scotland.[1] In Southern Ireland, Wesley was able to establish Societies, but despite his utmost endeavours he could not build up a strong body of Methodists. He was thwarted by the strength of the Roman Catholic Church. In Northern Ireland he met with much more success and Methodism spread rapidly. The prophet of Methodism in Wales had been Howell Harris, and by his unwearied labours he changed the face of the whole Principality. He found it nominally Anglican and left it aggressively Nonconformist. He was influenced more by Whitefield than Wesley, and the Welsh became Calvinistic Methodists. Even to-day, the Calvinistic Methodists in Wales far outnumber any other Methodist body. Congregationalism is numerically its strongest ally. Methodism was weak in Salop, Westmorland, Rutland, Cambridge, Huntingdon, Hereford, and Dorset. It was not much stronger in Cumberland, Derbyshire, Nottinghamshire, Suffolk, Essex and Devon. Methodism was strongest in manufacturing and industrial counties such as Staffordshire, Durham, Northumberland, Lancashire, Yorkshire, Middlesex and Cornwall. Thus it had no foothold in some counties, and in others its influence was greater than any other religious body. The purely agricultural regions of England were left almost unvisited and Wesley and his followers devoted themselves to larger centres of population. In his tours Wesley passed through Wiltshire, Hampshire and Surrey in a few days, but he devoted a month at a time to Cornwall or the district round Newcastle and Bristol. There is no record of Charles Wesley speaking in either Hampshire, Surrey or Wiltshire, except Devizes. In what was called the 'Wilderness' of the Southern Counties there were five hundred parishes that had no Methodist chapel.[2] At the time of Wesley's death, all Hampshire, and great parts of Surrey and Sussex, formed one Circuit. Portsmouth was the head of the Circuit, and there were three preachers and four hundred and thirty members. In 1811 there were only seventy-two members in the Sussex mission and fifty-

[1] *New History of Methodism*, Vol. I, p. 369.
[2] W. W. Pocock, *History of Wesleyan Methodism in some of the Southern Counties*, 1895.

five in the Chichester mission.¹ In 1789, Oxfordshire, Gloucestershire, and Worcestershire had 650, 381, and 235 members respectively. In the whole of Kent there were only 611 members.

The few members are not to be accounted for by the sparseness of the population. As a writer has pointed out, Bedfordshire, Leicestershire, Cornwall and Lincolnshire were scarcely more populated than the Southern Counties and yet Methodism had a much firmer hold in these areas.² The reason is that Methodism did not reach so effectively the peasant population bound to the fields, nor did it reach the tenant farmers, nor did it reach the country squires. The countryside with its tradition of parsonage and manor offered Methodism fewest opportunities of advance. There is hardly a reference in the *Journal* to the agricultural community, except in one place where Wesley said he had thought much on the encomiums bestowed on a country life.

'How have all the learned world cried out "O fortunati nimium sua si bona norint Agricolae!" But after all what a flat contradiction is this to universal experience! See that little house under the wood by the riverside, there is rural life in perfection. How happy then is the farmer that lives there. Let us take a detail of his happiness. He rises with or before the sun, calls his servants, looks to his swine and cows, then his stable and barns. He sees to the ploughing and sowing of his ground in Winter or in Spring. In Summer and Autumn he hurries and sweats among his mowers and reapers. And where is his happiness in the meantime? Which of these employments do we envy, or do we envy the delicate repast that succeeds which the poet so languishes for?

O quando faba, Pythagoras cognata simulque
Uncta satis pingui ponentur oluscula lardo!

'Oh, the happiness of eating beans well greased with fat bacon! Nay, and cabbage too!—Was Horace in his senses when he talked thus, or the servile herd of his imitators? Our eyes and ears may convince us there is not a less happy body of men in all England than the country farmers. In general, their life is supremely dull; and it is usually unhappy too. For of all the people in the kingdom they are most discontented; seldom satisfied either with God or man.'³

Wesley spoke of the farm labourers in even more scathing terms. He said the generality of English peasants were not only grossly stupid in the arts of this life but even more in regard to religion and

¹ *ibid.*
² *ibid.*
³ *Journal*, Vol. V, November 5, 1766.

the life to come. He said that if a countryman were questioned about faith, repentance, holiness, or true religion, he would not be able to give an intelligible answer. He would know just as much about the North-East Passage. Wesley said they could not practise what they did not know. Since religion was not even in their heads it could not be in their hearts and lives. He declared there was not the least savour of religion either in their temper or conversation, and that they were on the same level as a Turk or a Heathen.[1]

Even in counties that were largely agricultural such as Lincolnshire, Bedfordshire and Leicestershire, Methodism only touched the craftsmen, artisans, freeholders, and yeomanry.[2] In the Conference membership returns 1791, the Methodist Circuit was sometimes co-terminous with the county boundaries. This was the case with Sussex, Oxfordshire, Gloucestershire and Worcestershire. These counties were mainly agricultural. Circuits with over a thousand members were industrial towns in almost every case. The list was—London, Bristol, Redruth, St. Ives, Birmingham, Burslem, Macclesfield, Manchester, Bolton, Liverpool, Colne, Nottingham, Sheffield, Leeds, Birstal, Bradford, Halifax, Isle of Man, and Sunderland. The large numbers in the Redruth and St. Ives Circuits were drawn from the industrial population and principally from the tin miners. It is a legitimate deduction that Methodism drew its strength from the industrial and manufacturing sections of the community. By 1815 a slight increase had been made in the agricultural and pastoral counties but in the new centres of population there was a very large increase of members. The Conference of 1806 in commenting on the increase of 8,000 new members and 50 chapels within the year, spoke particularly of the increase in the manufacturing districts, where, said the Conference, multitudes had been converted to God.

In the period 1789 to 1815 certain Circuits had increased to over a thousand members. They were Bramley, Wakefield, Dewsbury, Epworth, York, Hull, Darlington, Barnard Castle, Newcastle and Shields. Apart from Epworth these were all Circuits in the Northern industrial counties.[3]

[1] 'Doctrine of Original Sin.' *Works*, Vol. IX, p. 225.
[2] W. W. Pocock, *History of Wesleyan Methodism in some of the Southern Counties*.
[3] Numbers given in the *Minutes of Conference* for the remainder of the middle period show the same process. Methodism increased rapidly in industrial areas and progressed very slowly in agricultural districts.

Whilst the strength of Methodism lay in the Northern industrial areas, it had captured some, but not the bulk, of the workers. Its attitude to social, economic and political questions, caused it to be regarded with a certain distrust.[1] Many workers already attached to Methodism seceded later to Primitive Methodism.

Methodism had its largest number of adherents in the new middle class which was being evolved out of the Industrial Revolution. These were people who by thrift and unceasing industry had risen from the lower classes. The very fact that in the early nineteenth century pew rents had become an accepted feature of Methodist chapels, showed the new status of the Society. In Durham and Northumberland Methodists had amongst their number—tradesmen, the new masters and professional men. The pitmen who attended Methodist meetings went largely to Primitive Methodist chapels. This was partly true in other industrial areas. Wesleyan Methodism still had large numbers of the poorer people but it ceased to exercise its old authority over the working classes. Richard Carlile refused to believe that a sect which issued thousands of pamphlets on the shortcomings of Tom Paine, and said not a word about the vices of the Bishop of Clogher could be a true ally of the working man. He said that the Society was fast becoming wealthy and powerful.[2] This was written by a foe but it represented a general impression. It was a fulfilment of what Wesley had prophesied in the latter years of his life.

Methodism had no influence over the aristocracy. In Wesley's writings there were many slighting references to the gentry and nobility. He bitterly begrudged the two hours he spent at Lady ——'s house. He said it needed great grace to converse with great people and one would willingly be excused.[3] It was in the same frame of mind that he left the House of Lords after spending two or three hours there. 'I had frequently heard that this was the most venerable assembly in England. But how was I disappointed! What is a Lord but a sinner born to die.'[4] When at the end of his life he thought of such churches as Bethesda and Lady Huntingdon's chapel, he marvelled at the condescension of God in providing places of worship where delicate hearers could hear doctrines set

[1] cf. The Chapter on 'The Industrial Revolution.'
[2] *The Republican*, August 1822 and September 1823.
[3] *Journal*, April 21, 1758.
[4] *ibid.*, January 25, 1785.

off with pretty trifles.[1] He avowed that much money need not imply much sense, nor need a good estate imply a good understanding. 'A gay coat may cover a bad heart, and a fair peruke may adorn a weak head.'[2] His *Manners of the Present Times* (1782) was a strong indictment of the sloth and luxury of the rich. He said that people of fashion could hardly huddle on their clothes before eight or nine o'clock in the morning, and some of them not before twelve, and when they had actually risen

> They waste away,
> In gentle inactivity the day.

He was horrified at young healthy men who were too lazy either to walk or ride, but who lolled in their carriages daily and could not make their carriages sufficiently comfortable.

From the outset there was no attempt to attract the aristocracy. Wesley corresponded with some titled people, and was on friendly terms with Lords North and Dartmouth; but there were no aristocrats in the Methodist Society. Those of the aristocracy who were religiously minded, associated themselves with the Evangelical party in the Church of England. Such influential statesmen as Lords Teignmouth and Liverpool were members of the movement. The Church was said to be the praying section of the Tory party, and that was true of the Evangelicals. What Methodism accomplished for the middle classes, the Evangelical party accomplished for the upper classes of the country. This comparison does not overlook the philanthropic enterprises of the Evangelicals nor their concern for the education of the poor.

Methodism had two sets of critics from the nation at large. One objection was the menace of Methodism to the Church of England. How real were these fears can be seen from Leigh Hunt's long pamphlet *The Folly and Danger of Methodism*, and Sidmouth's determined attempt to restrict the activities of the Methodist Society.

The second objection to Methodism was based on its narrowness of outlook. One writer spoke of 'the gloom of a life which had the austerities of a Trappist and in which even a smile was forbidden.'[3] The view was distorted but it showed how Methodism appeared to

---

[1] *Journal*, April 10, 1789.
[2] 'The Doctrine of Original Sin.' *Works*, Vol. IX, p. 235.
[3] Richard Carlile, *The Republican*, September 19, 1823.

unfriendly outsiders. Even some who were friendly to Methodists felt their attitude to recreations and amusements to be too uncompromising and wrote pamphlets advising Methodists to countenance dancing and the theatre.

Despite the unpopularity of Methodism with many people, it had a profound influence over the whole nation during the Napoleonic period. The two major happenings of that time were the War with Napoleon and the repressive conduct of the Government at home. Methodism gave valuable support both to the prosecution of the war and to the management of Home affairs.

It must not be thought that Methodists sanctioned war as such. Some of the strongest words uttered against the barbarity and futility of war were written by John Wesley. He said, speaking of the War of American Independence:

'See! Here are some thousands of our brave countrymen gathered together on this plain; they are followed by the most tender and feeling emotions of wives, children, and an innumerable multitude of their thoughtful, humane, and sympathizing countrymen. Then turn your eyes and behold a superior number at a little distance, of their brethren, "flesh of their flesh, and bone of their bone," who only a few years since emigrated to the dreary wilds of America. These also are followed with the most tender feelings of wives, children, and countrymen. See, they advance towards each other, well prepared with every instrument of death! But what are they going to do? To shoot each other through the head or heart; to stab and butcher each other, and hasten (it is to be feared) one another into everlasting burnings. Why so? What harm have they done to one another? Why, none at all. Most of them are entire strangers to each other. But a matter is in dispute relative to the mode of taxation. So these countrymen, children of the same parents, are to murder each other with all possible haste, to prove who is in the right. Now, what an argument is this! What a method of proof! What an amazing way of deciding controversies! But so it is; and O what horrors attend on it! At what price is the decision made! By the blood and wounds of thousands, the burning cities, ravaging and laying waste the country.'[1]

In his treatise 'The Doctrine of Original Sin' he summed up the causes of war and showed in a scathing manner that none were sufficiently adequate to justify the outbreak of hostilities. He bewailed the fact that if the King of France had a quarrel with the King of England, Frenchmen and Englishmen were to kill as many of each other as possible in order to prove who was in the right. He thought there was a shocking want of common understanding and humanity

[1] 'Seasonable address to the inhabitants of Great Britian.' *Works*, Vol. IX, p. 121.

in the world for two nations ever to think of such a method of decision.¹

Wesley's views on war represented those of his successors. When England engaged in the war with France however, and it was no longer possible for peaceful councils to prevail, Methodists gave unswerving support to the Government. There is a close parallel in this action with Wesley's attitude to the War of American Independence. Wesley used all his influence before the outbreak of war to urge a peaceful consideration of the matters in dispute. He tried to hold the balances evenly and to show that each side had a strong case to present. Once war broke out, and it was impossible to counsel peace, Wesley threw himself into the advocacy of the war and became one of the staunchest supporters of the Government. When war became inevitable it is not difficult to understand why Methodists regarded it as a righteous crusade. The French Revolution was associated in their minds with infidelity. Democracy in any case they viewed with distrust.

Napoleon with his ambitious schemes seemed to them a veritable Anti-Christ. Added to hatred of the new order in France was love of the existing system of Government in England. It was for these reasons that Methodism gave warmest support to the war once England had committed itself to the struggle. A much respected Methodist minister spoke of a Jacobin as a 'political madman' and Napoleon as the 'Corsican Ogre.'² According to an article in the *Quarterly Review* Methodists regarded Napoleon, in apocalyptic terms, as the Beast.³ John Braithwaite published a sermon he had delivered on the victory of Nelson at Trafalgar.⁴ It was a paean of thanksgiving for the defeat of the enemy. Throughout the whole Methodist Society, prayers of thanksgiving were offered after the rebellion in Ireland had failed, and after the sea victories of Nelson. The Conference ordered a prayer meeting every Friday, and a fast day every month for the nation in its peril. This was continued until the close of the war.

Methodists made good fighters and gained a reputation on the land. The Conference of 1803 denounced all those who sought to evade military service by gaining a preacher's licence. As to their

---

[1] 'Doctrine of Original Sin.' *Works*, Vol. IX, p. 222.
[2] *Proceedings of Wesley Historical Society* (1901-1903).
[3] *Quarterly Review*, November 1810.
[4] *Sermons* (1788-1852).

THE NAPOLEONIC PERIOD

service on the water the following extract from the letter of a naval officer bears witness. 'There was a set of fellows called Methodists on board the *Victory*, Lord Nelson's ship, and these men never wanted swearing at. The dogs were the best seamen on board. Every man knew his duty and every man did his duty. They used to meet together and sing hymns and nobody dared to molest them. . . . These men were the only fellows I ever knew do their duty without swearing and I will do them the justice to say they did it.'[1] The *Evangelical Magazine* printed a letter from a seaman to his mother in which he spoke of the courage shown by Methodists in various naval actions.[2]

As Methodists supported the war abroad, so they supported the Government at home. The vigorous repression of all reform propaganda was heartily approved by a Society which strove to stamp out all democratic sentiments in its members and expelled any known republican. In the pastoral letter of 1793, the Conference declared that it had been suggested that some Methodists were defective in loyalty. The Conference rejoined that if any such men could be produced and evidence of their guilt supplied, they would be instantly cut off from the Connexion as unworthy of any office in the Church of God and as enemies to their King and Country. The letter concluded that Methodists held their Sovereign Lord, King George in high estimation, loved their Country and its Constitution, and that its ministers were willing to support their King and Country with all they had and were.

The Conference of 1812 after considering the benefits Englishmen enjoyed under their present Government deplored the principles which had caused so much unrest and cautioned Methodists against the agitation. Sorrow was expressed for the poverty and distress which prevailed, but Methodists were urged to bear patiently what could not be remedied. This belief in uncomplaining patience led official Methodism to disapprove of the Reform movements in the North and to support the action of the Government.

One cannot easily exaggerate the help Methodism gave to the Government in the early nineteenth century by this attitude of uncritical admiration and unswerving loyalty. Its ultimate effect was to strengthen in a dangerous fashion the forces of reaction and conservatism, but its immediate effect was to enable the Govern-

[1] *Methodist Magazine*, October 1808.
[2] *Evangelical Magazine*, Vol. XVII, p. 343.

ment to prosecute the war abroad, without any feeling of insecurity or half-heartedness at home. From this point of view Methodism rendered magnificent service.

Within its ranks were individuals who in their liberalism were to deviate widely from the parent body. They were to be the precursors of ever-increasing numbers, and their influence was to modify greatly the Toryism of the Society. But in this period of national crisis, Methodists still uttered with one voice the praise of the King and the Constitution.

CHAPTER II

JABEZ BUNTING: THE SIGNIFICANCE OF HIS CAREER

THROUGHOUT the period covered by this book, Jabez Bunting was the dominant personality in Wesleyan Methodism. When one of Wesley's preachers called at Monyash on his way to Liverpool to embark for America, he preached from the unusual text 'And Jabez was more honourable than his Brethren' (I Chron. iv. 9). The sermon made a lasting impression on Mary Redfern, a young woman in the congregation. Years later she became Mary Bunting and the first son of the marriage was born in Manchester May 13, 1779. He was christened Jabez and dedicated by his mother to the service of God. In time he was sent to the best school in Manchester and became friendly with the son of a well-known physician called Dr. Percival. When his education at school was finished, the doctor received young Bunting into his household and instructed him. In return Bunting did secretarial work for the doctor. Bunting, however, was not a pupil only, he was a member of the family. Between 1795 and 1799 the house became his home. In the latter year he was received as an itinerant preacher and appointed to the Salford Circuit. Twelve years after Wesley's death (1803) he was received into full connexion and was sent to preach in a London Circuit. This brought him into contact with the outstanding preachers of Methodism and some of its most important laymen. It also enabled his great gifts to be early recognized and appreciated. His correspondence with Miss Maclardie, later to be his wife, shows how heavy his preaching duties were at this time.

In 1804 he had another and a greater opportunity of showing his worth. After Wesley's death Dr. Thomas Coke became the most important figure in Methodism. He held the rank of Superintendent in America and all the missionary activities of Methodism were under his direction. He was promptly appointed Secretary of the Conference when Wesley died. The choice seemed inevitable. In 1795, and again in 1805, he became President of the Conference.

Meanwhile his constant journeyings and many responsibilities made it impossible for him to discharge his duties as Secretary efficiently. Indeed, for several years he did not even join his signature as Secretary with that of the President in the authentication of the *Minutes of Conference*.[1] Members of the Conference became weary of the farce. Coke had no time to attend to the accounts of the Book-Room nor even the Missionary accounts. The confusion steadily increased until the Rev. Robert Lomas was asked (1804) to try to bring order out of chaos. He called on Jabez Bunting to assist him, and the young man began to 'plough through acres of figures.'[2] The Conference of 1806 made a determined attempt to end the unreal situation and Coke only just succeeded in retaining his Secretaryship. Benson gained almost the same number of votes. It was decided to appoint an assistant secretary and Jabez Bunting was chosen. He said in a letter to his mother written at this time that whilst it meant added work, it enabled him to occupy a capital station in the Conference, sitting close to the President's chair where everything could be heard and seen. He told her that the position would enable him to gain considerable information on Methodist affairs.

In the meantime he had already assisted in founding the *Eclectic Review*—a paper which for the next half-century was to have great influence in Nonconformist circles. From this time onwards Bunting was an outstanding figure in his Church. He and his closest friend Robert Newton are the only Methodist ministers who have occupied the Presidential chair on four occasions. When he first became President in 1820 Bunting had only travelled twenty-one years in the ministry.[3]

There were at least four distinct ways in which he served the Connexion. Throughout his long ministry he laboured to improve the organization of Methodism. The detailed schedules which have to be filled up annually by Superintendent ministers are largely the fruit of his many suggestions. Admission to the Legal Hundred had been a matter of seniority. In 1814 through Bunting's influence, Conference decided that one in every four vacancies to the Legal Hundred should be filled by young preachers who had travelled at least fourteen years. Perhaps his greatest contribution to the

---

[1] See J. H. Rigg, *Jabez Bunting*, p. 84.
[2] 'Jabez Bunting' (*Methodist Worthies*, Vol. II, p. 253).
[3] He was President in 1820, 1828, 1836, and 1844.

administration of Methodism was his plea that laymen should have equal place with ministers on Connexional Committees. At first he met with determined opposition from senior ministers but in the end his influence prevailed. As a result of his counsel the preparatory work of Conference was done by mixed committees whose reports were submitted for the approval of Conference. There are many other details of organized Methodism which owe their inception to him. The use of the title 'Reverend,' the laying on of hands at ordination, the placing of various Connexional funds on a permanent basis, all helped to give Methodism separate status as a Church.[1]

Secondly Bunting rendered great service to the Missionary Society. It might almost be said that he founded it. When he was appointed to the Leeds Circuit in 1813 he helped to start District Missionary committees and meetings. With the first meeting at Leeds the Missionary Society may be said to have started.[2] When we speak of the valuable work done by Richard Watson for the cause of Foreign Missions, it is well to remember that he was encouraged to devote his mind and energies to the work by the influence and close friendship of Jabez Bunting. When Bunting became Connexional Editor after Benson's death in 1821, Watson succeeded him as Secretary of the Wesleyan Missionary Society in Hatton Garden, London. In that office he was assisted by the continued sympathy and kindness of Bunting. The two men appeared together on many missionary platforms and led the Methodist crusade against slavery.

A third way in which Bunting helped Methodism was by his preaching. To-day his sermons would seem rather dull. The language is sonorous and stately but rather chilling in its effect on the reader. In his own day, however, his only equal in popular regard was Robert Newton. Robert Hall described Bunting's style of preaching as 'a limpid stream of classic elegance,' whilst William Arthur spoke of it as 'a union of reason, simplicity and vehemence.'[3] If he was a prince of the pulpit he was also a master of assemblies: none excelled him in debate. He had not only the power of making his points clearly and effectively, but of silencing an opponent by pungent criticism and occasionally by 'a terrible moment' of sarcasm.

[1] J. H. Rigg, *Jabez Bunting*, pp. 101, 102.
[2] *Methodist Worthies*, Vol. II, p. 256.
[3] J. H. Rigg, *Jabez Bunting*, p. 115.

In one last respect Bunting rendered notable service to Methodism. He was a great advocate of wider opportunities for education. When in 1811 the Conference appointed him to the Halifax Circuit, he saw the possibility of a school for preachers' children at Woodhouse Grove, and through his influence the property was secured. He realized the imperative need for an educated ministry and laboured to convince his fellow-Methodists. In time his perseverance was rewarded, and in 1834 a Theological Institution was founded. Against his wishes he was made the first President of the Institution (people were suspicious of the word 'College') and remained so till his death. His duties actually were those of visitation and supervision rather than of actual lecturing. Through him, however, more than through any other man, the value of education for the ministry was realized in the Methodist Church.

It has been necessary to stress the supreme importance of Bunting in the first half of the nineteenth century, in order to show how greatly his political views influenced his Church. In a denomination which could boast of many outstanding personalities he was *facile princeps*. The church polity of Bunting was progressive. He valued the co-operation of laymen on committees, he extended the control of District Meetings over finance and he gave Quarterly Meetings a legal constitution.[1] But his radicalism in Church government had definite limits. He left the ultimate authority strictly in the pastorate. 'The Kilhamite practice of proposing names at a leaders' meeting is one of our abominations.' No freely elected and therefore strictly representative laymen sat on Church committees.[2] His opponents saw in him the apostle of ministerial authority and dominance.

In politics Bunting was strongly sympathetic to Toryism. He regarded Socialism as anti-Christian. He said that 'Methodism hates democracy as much as it hates sin.'[3] He set his face rigorously against the Luddites and showed no tolerance of their aims or methods. It was under his dictation that Conference recommended all those in want and distress to seek their deliverance from God and not from men. They were to have courage and patience, confident in the knowledge that the Lord would be mindful of his own. Those who took part in the Reform agitations received no mercy

[1] *New History of Methodism*, Vol. I, p. 408.
[2] *ibid.*, Vol. I, p. 528.
[3] See *Methodism as it is*, 1863, by James Everett.

from him. When anxious souls like Jeremiah Bettrell wanted to warn official Methodism against the implication of certain Methodists in the Reform meetings, it was to Bunting they wrote, and from him that they received word to deal rigorously with those in their Societies suspected of being Reformers. When the six Dorsetshire labourers had been convicted for joining an agricultural trade union Bunting was too busy to see Jane Davis who had travelled to London on purpose to see him and plead their case. His only regret was to think that they were Methodists, and he never attempted to secure pardon or mitigation of their sentence. They were sent out to Botany Bay as convicts to serve a seven years' sentence. On arrival at Hobart, 'Van Diemens Land' (Tasmania), George Loveless was sent to work on the roads in a chain gang. His friends were working on farms in Australia. Brine was wretchedly unhappy with a master who behaved like a slave driver. The two Stanfields, James Loveless and James Hammett were not altogether miserable, but they had the pain of separation from their loved ones and the long laborious hours on a farm with feet fettered in chains. The eventual release of the six men came through the untiring agitation of Doctor Thomas Wakley. The attitude of Bunting may be understood from the fact that he wrote a letter to the Tory candidate who was opposing Wakley in the Finsbury Park Division, and assured him of his strong support. Wakley was elected despite Bunting, and presented a petition signed by 130,000 people, asking for the return of the Dorsetshire labourers. This he followed by a speech delivered on June 25, 1835, in which he pleaded the cause of the unfortunate men. *The Times* newspaper ordinarily had no sympathy with the trade unionists. It regarded combinations of workmen against their masters as wrong. In this instance, however, it departed from its customary position. It denounced the severity of the sentence passed on the men and the injustice of procuring by an Act of Parliament, applicable to the men of the Army and Navy, a condemnation of civilians.[1] The government realized the weight of the agitation and an order was sent out for the release of the six men. From the beginning to the end of the agitation, Methodism had shown no official sympathy and offered no aid. Bunting, who

---

[1] Owen Rattenbury, *Flame of Freedom*, p. 158. If the Jane Davis story is not true in fact, it is most certainly true in principle. Bunting took no steps to help them.

heartily disliked combinations of workmen, lent his prestige to the government and studiously ignored the agitation.

Bunting was a Tory. His complete hold over his people meant that his political as well as his religious views were acceptable to the great majority of Methodists. However great his gifts, and however strong his personality, he could not establish his ascendancy if his politics were unpopular. The story of the protests against his rule is in one aspect the story of the rise of Radicalism within the Methodist Society. For many years there was no audible opposition. Then came the first signs of revolt, and finally came the agitation which swept through Methodism and split the Connexion. It is not unreasonable to suppose that until 1830 (the year of revolutions) his views represented those of the Methodist people. His strength on the platform and in Conference came not only because of his powers of utterance, but because he was uttering the mind of the Society. After 1830 it became noticeable that an opposition existed. It did not carry the assent of Methodism and therefore was always in a hopeless minority. The significant thing is that it was present. Bunting could easily override it, but he could not ignore it.

Gradually opposition was offered by more violent and less respectful opponents. It was the more dangerous because it was so largely anonymous, and relied on the pen and not the spoken word. Bunting was not able therefore to stamp on it in debate. It was dangerous because it was offered not by the great personalities of Methodism but by the ordinary ministers and laity. It marked the rise of an opposition which was so powerful that it made obvious the existence of a Radicalism wholly opposed to the Churchmanship and Toryism of Bunting. Methodism was no longer secure in his grasp. He still represented the views of the majority, but by 1848 the Society could no longer be described as Conservative in Church government and in politics. There was a dominant Conservatism strongly tempered by a virile minority of Radicals. And it was fairly certain with whom the future lay.

The first real attempt to oppose Bunting came from Samuel Warren. It was actuated mainly by his personal motives of jealousy and dislike. Warren was as zealous for the education of the ministry as Bunting himself. He advocated strongly the need for a Theological Institution. The project was approved by the Conference of 1834 and Jabez Bunting was appointed President of the Institution.

This appointment greatly displeased Warren and caused him to change his whole attitude to the scheme. He said, 'the proposed appointments would throw additional power into the hands of individuals.'[1] He doubtless felt that Bunting had too much power as it was, but his attack was not disinterested. He held a Doctorate in Divinity from a Scots university and fondly imagined that he would be chosen to preside over the Institution. Thus jealousy and disappointment added bitterness to his opposition. He denounced the ambition of Bunting in Conference, and then published his speech in pamphlet form. When the President of the Conference sent him a friendly letter of remonstrance, he replied by a second letter in which he reiterated his charges, and proposed certain reforms. His final step was to declare that the President had no power over his Circuit in Manchester. The District Meeting had no option but to suspend him from exercising his ministerial functions. He sought restitution by lawsuit in which his knowledge of law and his powers of debate were fully shown. Unfortunately for him, Lord Chancellor Lyndhurst decided in favour of Conference on all points.

The interesting feature of his agitation was that it led to the formation of the Wesleyan Methodist Association. He became its first President (1835). The Association did not diverge from the parent body in doctrine but only in organization. The Assembly was elected from Circuits who sent ministers and laymen in proportion to their number. Following the lead already given by Warren in Manchester, Circuits were given independence in their own affairs.

Thus, quite apart from the personal motives which influenced Warren, there were many who seceded with him because they disliked the autocracy of Bunting and the Conservatism of Wesleyan government, and desired to set up a more democratic organization. They were regarded as Radicals by the Connexion they had left. This was not, of course, the only secession in these years. In 1827 the trustees of Brunswick Chapel, Leeds, decided to ask permission for an organ to be built. This was contrary to the desire of the majority of the congregation and the District Meeting decided to reject the application. Unfortunately they left the way open for the trustees to appeal to Conference. Bunting's sympathies were with the trustees and not the people. He had in any case a strong liking

[1] *New History of Methodism*, Vol. I, p. 517.

for liturgical services and for ceremony and dignity in public worship. The project of an organ appealed to him and Conference acceded to the trustees' request. This decision not only overruled the District Meeting, but rode rough-shod over the desires of the Brunswick Circuit as a whole. The chief blame was fixed on Bunting. It was said that the Leeds organ cost £1,000 and 1,000 members. The seceders styled themselves 'Protestant Methodists,' and when in 1836 they united with the Wesleyan Association they had several thousand members.[1] These early secessions were prompted partly by dislike of Bunting and what he symbolized. They were, however, not so significant as the later secession of 1849. They were local in character and small in numbers. They did not indicate any strong opposition in Methodism to Bunting and his Conservatism. The important feature at this time was the growth of opposition among individual Methodists of high standing. Among the laity were John Petrie, a close friend and sympathizer of Cobden and Bright in the Corn Law agitations, and Robert Eckitt (later a minister) who felt compelled to leave Wesleyan Methodism and associate themselves with Warren's movement. Among the Wesleyan ministry three prominent men, Joseph Fowler (father of the first Lord Wolverhampton), Joseph Beaumont (a Doctor of Medicine) and James Everett, were willing to oppose Bunting in Conference when occasion demanded it. The important point is that all three men were radical in their views.

Neither of the three ministers, separately or conjointly, were a match for Bunting, but gradually their point of view was adopted by an ever-increasing number. On occasions Bunting's own son, William Maclardie Bunting, the hymn-writer, opposed him in debate. William Atherton (father of the first Methodist attorney-general) was another doughty opponent of Bunting when occasion required. Amongst the younger men William Arthur was always ready to try a fall with Bunting, even though the two men respected and even loved each other deeply.

Not until the Flysheets agitation of 1848 did it become apparent that the opposition was widespread and violent.[2] In this third phase the leadership of the opposition passed to other hands. Bunting was no longer opposed by men who respected and admired him but by those who saw him only as a stumbling block to progress.

[1] *New History of Methodism*, Vol. I, p. 516.
[2] Actually the first volume of Flysheets was printed in 1841.

The opposition used the pen rather than the platform. Between 1844 and 1848 four pamphlets appeared without the printer's name and each closed with the words 'By order of the Corresponding Committee for detecting, exposing and correcting abuses.'[1] They declaimed against ministerial authority and the misuse of the presidential chair. Democratic reforms in Church government were proposed. The strength of the pamphlets lay in the personal and violent nature of the attack. Other ministers apart from Bunting were criticized, sometimes unfairly, for their supposed belief in autocracy. The pamphlets were sent at first to every minister, but later they were reprinted and had a very wide circulation. Sometimes the reply to these attacks was not temperate. 'Papers on Wesleyan Matters,' though anonymous, defended the maligned ministers with some acerbity of spirit. It was in the pages of *The Watchman* that the best defence appeared. Three men were suspect from the first. Samuel Dunn was a voluminous writer and a great Evangelist. His paper, *The Wesley Banner*, was always Evangelical in tone, but he frequently used its pages to support the point of view adopted by the Flysheets. William Griffith was known as a Radical in politics as well as Church polity. He wrote articles pleading for social reform, and reform in Methodist organization, in the *Wesleyan Times*.

Chief suspicion fell on James Everett. He had opposed the scheme for the Theological Institution and for Centenary celebrations. A year after the Centenary appeared an anonymous work, *Wesleyan Takings*, which was popularly attributed to him. It consisted of a series of clever sketches of Wesleyan ministers. He took great care to paint the wart on their noses, but he was not always so careful to indicate the finer qualities of their character. For years he had been known as a strong opponent of Bunting and a leading advocate of reform. No one was so ready a writer and versifier, and in the estimation of the majority no one was more likely to have had some share in the writing of the Flysheets than himself.

Dunn, Griffith, and himself were among the thirty-six ministers who refused to sign a declaration that they were not involved in the publication of the Flysheets, nor were sympathetic with their aims. He and his friends were summoned to the Manchester Conference of 1849. They were questioned about the Flysheets but refused to give any direct answer. Certain ministers (Burdsall, Walton, George

[1] *New History of Methodism*, Vol. I, p. 530.

and Bromley) were censured, but Everett, Dunn and Griffith were expelled. No charge was brought against their character or their devotion to work, nor could it definitely be proved that they were responsible for the Flysheets. Everett was expelled for 'contumacy,' and Dunn and Griffiths for not stopping the *Wesley Banner* and for sending contributions to the *Wesleyan Times*.

These expulsions would not of themselves be so important were it not for the agitation which followed. Very significantly the three ministers made their appeal to the people—'A yet auguster thing than Parliament, King or Conference.'[1] In all the big centres great gatherings sympathetic to the expelled ministers were held. Newspapers took up their cause, and bitter feeling was aroused. A conciliatory attitude was essential if peace was to be preserved. Unhappily the majority of Wesleyan ministers were inflexible in their determination to expel all sympathizers with the three ministers, and all who advocated reforms. The expulsions and secessions amounted in all to 100,000 members. The President of the Conference refused to meet delegates from various groups of reformers. Petitions sent to Conference were ignored. For seven Conferences (1850 to 1856) delegates from the reformers tried to obtain a hearing, and to effect, if possible, a reconciliation. From the claims they made it is obvious how radical was their point of view. They desired that the expelled should be reinstated and that the laws which made such expulsion possible should be repealed. They asked that the people's delegates should be represented in Church courts. They desired that the members of a Church and not the minister should control the exclusion or admission of members and the appointment of officers. They did not wish to limit the power of Conference but they did consider that local courts should be independent in their internal affairs.[2]

Although at the time their efforts were fruitless, it is not unreasonable to suppose that later reforms in the parent body derived their original inspiration from those days. Much of what the reformers sought came to pass. Laymen were admitted to the Wesleyan Conference in 1877. Greater publicity was given to the proceedings of Conference, and the old intransigent attitude of ministers was never again adopted. The Flysheet agitation closed a second period of Methodist history. Within that period there were

[1] *New History of Methodism*, Vol. I, p. 533.
[2] *ibid.*, p. 536.

JABEZ BUNTING: THE SIGNIFICANCE OF HIS CAREER 161

three phases of development. For the first quarter of the century at least Methodism was predominantly conservative in social and political ideas. There were exceptions, but Methodism as a whole was devoutly attached to King and Constitution and to things as they were. Whilst Congregationalists and Calvinistic Methodists were calling their chapels by names derived from the Bible, Methodism was building great chapels in the big centres of the north and calling them after the House of Brunswick. These Brunswick chapels were always outstanding in their size and importance. The Toryism of Bunting was an accurate repetition of the political opinions of his people.

Between 1830 and 1844 there was a growing opposition to Bunting which, quite reasonably, might be called the growth of a radical sentiment. As is so often the case, it began with leading men and was gradually adopted by the commonalty. The radical ideas of the few became in time the possession of the many. The third period began in 1844 and reached its climax in the revolutionary years of 1848 and 1849. One cannot separate the Radicalism which split Methodism from manifestations of the same spirit on the continent and in the great Chartist movement of our own country. Indeed many of the Radicals who opposed the rule of Bunting and his friends were friendly to Chartism. The opposition of 1848 was significant because it revealed the widespread growth of Radicalism within the Wesleyan connexion. After 1850 Wesleyan Methodism could no longer be described as Tory in its politics and closely attached to the Church. Finding its strength drawn almost wholly from the commercial and industrial classes it had become increasingly Nonconformist in its sympathies, and Radical in its outlook. The old connexion with the Church was almost forgotten. The final revolt against Bunting and his friends was much more than a personal animus. It was a new attitude to politics and social reform. If Liberalism in the second half of the nineteenth century owed much to Nonconformist support, it was because Nonconformity had been reinforced by a new and most powerful ally. In the middle period of Methodism the dominating figure was Jabez Bunting the Tory. In the last period of Methodism the dominating figure was Hugh Price Hughes, the Radical.

L

APPENDIX I

TABLE TO SHOW THE INCREASE OF METHODISM BETWEEN 1789 AND 1815

Names of Towns	Year 1789	Year 1791	Year 1815
London	2,680	2,950	6,350
Sussex	268	260	—
Kent	611	—	—
Colchester	290	145	245
Norwich }	730	580	675
Yarmouth }		—	670
Lynn	350	370	487
Bedford	237	500	300
Northampton	370	470	450
Oxfordshire	650	700	—
Gloucestershire	381	316	—
Worcestershire	235	288	—
Sarum	636	238	—
Isle of Jersey	294	316	—
Isle of Guernsey	105	222	—
Bradford-on-Avon	1,290	952	440
Bristol	2,203	1,562	2,120
Taunton	275	234	400
Tiverton	420	408	—
Bideford	83	150	—
Plymouth	805	816	490
St. Austell	785	950	850
Redruth	1,800	1,705	4,350
St. Ives	1,379	1,537	—
Pembroke	163	168	140
Glamorganshire	273	250	—
Brecon	202	116	—
Birmingham	1,260	1,600	1,280
Wolverhampton	548	612	460
Burslem	1,280	1,434	1,070
Macclesfield	1,060	1,140	1,030
Stockport	827	655	1,310
Manchester	2,050	2,090	2,800

Names of Towns	Year 1789	Year 1791	Year 1815
Bolton	1,080	1,160	1,390
Chester ⎫ Wirral ⎭	599	614	700
Liverpool	900	1,050	2,730
Blackburn	880	955	650
Colne	960	1,020	580
Leicester	622	768	663
Nottingham	840	1,000	1,359
Derby	742	785	780
Sheffield	1,670	1,690	2,228
Grimsby	609	583	620
Horncastle	640	638	710
Gainsborough	720	700	800
Epworth	670	710	1,000
Leeds	2,140	2,080	3,530
Wakefield	689	730	1,045
Huddersfield	866	780	1,012
Birstal	1,403	1,230	1,690
Bradford	1,075	1,095	1,800
Halifax	1,100	1,115	1,300
Keighley	1,330	900	850
Whitehaven	240	282	560
Isle of Man	2,569	2,500 Douglas	1,260
York	886	974	1,500
Pocklington	800	834	830
Hull	684	664	1,970
Scarborough	660	621	610
Whitby	611	545	760
Thirsk	660	629	830
Yarm	522	554	—
The Dales	1,060	986	—
Sunderland	1,240	1,250	1,600
Newcastle	1,000	780	1,250
Berwick ⎫ Dalkeith ⎭	142	—	—
Edinburgh	346	205	314
Ayr & Dumfries	80	—	—
Dumfries	—	44	36
Ayr & Kilmarnock	—	—	200
Dundee	137	157	70
Aberdeen	261	286	338

APPENDIX I

Names of Towns	Year 1789	Year 1791	Year 1815
Inverness	220	222	30
Chatham	—	280	—
Canterbury	—	296	570
Diss	—	310	410
Bury	—	160	590
Portsmouth	—	430	1,200
Shepton Mallet	—	950	740
Otley	—	560	480
Alnwick	—	300	—
Alnwick & Berwick	—	—	307
Glasgow	—	218	—
Glasgow, Paisley, &c.	—	—	1,111
Greenock & Port Glasgow	—	—	70
Campbelton	—	16	—
Kelso	—	31	—
Brentford	—	—	340
Windsor	—	—	26
Deptford	—	—	1,040
Leigh (Essex)	—	—	62
Chelmsford	—	—	98
Harwich	—	—	440
Ipswich	—	—	442
Huntingdon	—	—	350
St. Neots	—	—	316
Biggleswade	—	—	185
Newport-Pagnell	—	—	200
Ampthill	—	—	200
Leighton Buzzard	—	—	470
Luton	—	—	484
Reading	—	—	94
Chichester	—	—	96
Brighthelmstone	—	—	288
Rochester	—	—	1,100
Margate	—	—	265
Dover	—	—	396
Rye	—	—	930
Ashford	—	—	65
Sevenoaks	—	—	270
Maidstone	—	—	250
North Walsham	—	—	205
Lowestoft	—	—	370

Names of Towns	Year 1789	Year 1791	Year 1815
Framlington	—	—	256
Bungay	—	—	164
New Buckenham	—	—	360
Thetford	—	—	398
Bury St. Edmunds	—	—	195
Ely	—	—	350
Swaffham	—	—	270
Wisbeach	—	—	427
Walsingham	—	—	694
Oxford & High Wycombe	—	—	370
Whitchurch	—	—	218
Witney	—	—	240
Chipping Norton	—	—	240
Banbury	—	—	350
Brackley	—	—	373
Towcester	—	—	273
Daventry	—	—	359
Wellingborough	—	—	460
Kettering	—	—	120
Market Harborough	—	—	130
Salisbury	—	—	660
Shaftesbury	—	—	400
Poole	—	—	365
Isle of Wight	—	—	263
Southampton	—	—	485
Newbury	—	—	333
Hungerford	—	—	428
Guernsey { English	—	—	200
{ French	—	—	432
Jersey { English	—	—	180
{ French	—	—	671
Alderney { English	—	—	30
{ French	—	—	72
Plymouth Dock } Plymouth	—	—	1,232
Launceston	—	—	488
Stratton	—	—	214
Liskeard	—	—	769
Tavistock	—	—	400
Camelford	—	—	480
Kingsbridge	—	—	190

APPENDIX I

Names of Towns	Year 1789	Year 1791	Year 1815
Truro	—	—	2,800
Penzance & Scilly Islands	—	—	2,700
Helston	—	—	2,986
Exeter	—	—	745
S. Petherton	—	—	328
Axminster	—	—	192
Barnstaple	—	—	409
Dunster	—	—	139
Oakhampton	—	—	89
Ashburton	—	—	333
Brixham	—	—	250
Kingswood	—	—	350
Banwell	—	—	416
Bath	—	—	680
Frome	—	—	630
Bruton	—	—	90
Warminster	—	—	200
Stroud & Cirencester	—	—	378
Dursley	—	—	332
Downend	—	—	455
Gloucester	—	—	340
Cheltenham	—	—	124
Weymouth	—	—	264
Melksham	—	—	383
Midsomer Norton	—	—	730
Glastonbury	—	—	100
Haverfordwest	—	—	250
Carmarthen { English	—	—	113
Carmarthen { Welsh	—	—	190
Swansea { English	—	—	237
Swansea { Welsh	—	—	228
Merthyr Tydvil { English	—	—	153
Merthyr Tydvil { Welsh	—	—	228
Brecon { English	—	—	164
Brecon { Welsh	—	—	161
Monmouth	—	—	322
Cardiff	—	—	405
Newport	—	—	330
Llandilo	—	—	243
Cardigan	—	—	192
St. Davids	—	—	81

Names of Towns	Year 1789	Year 1791	Year 1815
Aberystwyth	—	—	333
Machynlleth	—	—	305
Dolgelly	—	—	366
Carnarvon	—	—	256
Pwllheli	—	—	210
Holyhead	—	—	188
Beaumaris	—	—	237
Llanrwst	—	—	290
Ruthin & Denbigh	—	—	325
Holywell	—	—	604
Llangollen	—	—	272
Llanfyllyn	—	—	265
Llanidloes	—	—	269
West Bromwich	—	—	170
Coleshill	—	—	30
Redditch	—	—	344
Wednesbury	—	—	1,130
Worcester	—	—	680
Evesham	—	—	307
Stourport	—	—	499
Dudley	—	—	1,340
Hinckley	—	—	530
Coventry	—	—	400
Shrewsbury	—	—	693
Broseley	—	—	683
Ludlow	—	—	320
Hereford	—	—	130
Ledbury	—	—	160
Kington	—	—	250
Newtown	—	—	246
Wrexham	—	—	298
Oswestry	—	—	115
Buxton	—	—	380
Congleton	—	—	469
Nantwich	—	—	570
Northwich	—	—	778
Newcastle-under-Lyme	—	—	920
Stafford	—	—	308
Leek	—	—	833
Warrington	—	—	600
Prescot	—	—	265

APPENDIX I

Names of Towns	Year 1789	Year 1791	Year 1815
Wigan	—	—	260
Ormskirk	—	—	231
Preston	—	—	760
Garstang	—	—	180
Lancaster	—	—	475
Salford	—	—	1,570
New Mills	—	—	665
Aston-under-Lyne	—	—	240
Oldham	—	—	780
Rochdale	—	—	870
Bacup	—	—	390
Haslingden	—	—	384
Burnley	—	—	580
Sowerby Bridge	—	—	970
Todmorden	—	—	1,450
Skipton	—	—	423
Clitheroe	—	—	400
Grassington	—	—	160
Addington	—	—	420
Bingley	—	—	800
Woodhouse Grove	—	—	830
Holmfirth	—	—	600
Bramley	—	—	1,240
Dewsbury	—	—	1,041
Pateley Bridge	—	—	500
Pontefract	—	—	700
Selby	—	—	600
Wetherby	—	—	570
Chesterfield	—	—	500
Bakewell	—	—	362
Bradwell	—	—	452
Rotherham	—	—	928
Doncaster	—	—	620
Barnsley	—	—	470
Denby, Nr. Huddersfield	—	—	410
Belper	—	—	850
Cromford	—	—	380
Retford	—	—	780
Ilkeston	—	—	400
Mansfield & Worksop	—	—	583
Newark	—	—	800

Names of Towns	Year 1789	Year 1791	Year 1815
Melton Mowbray	—	—	440
Ashby-de-la-Zouch	—	—	810
Burton & Lichfield	—	—	340
Uttoxeter	—	—	313
Loughborough	—	—	620
Stamford & Peterborough	—	—	460
Lincoln & Sleaford	—	—	980
Market Rasen	—	—	515
Louth	—	—	886
Alford	—	—	406
Spilsby	—	—	470
Boston	—	—	450
Spalding	—	—	250
Winterton	—	—	586
Patrington	—	—	376
Howden	—	—	630
Bridlington	—	—	785
Driffield	—	—	715
Pickering	—	—	519
Melton	—	—	600
Easingwold	—	—	640
Guisborough	—	—	650
Ripon	—	—	700
Darlington	—	—	1,190
Barnard Castle	—	—	1,340
Middleham	—	—	390
Tanfield	—	—	370
Richmond	—	—	970
Gateshead	—	—	924
Shields	—	—	1,700
Durham	—	—	710
Alston	—	—	500
Carlisle	—	—	377
Brough	—	—	252
Penrith	—	—	102
Kendal	—	—	309
Ulverstone	—	—	55
Ramsey	—	—	1,651
Dunbar & Haddington	—	—	55
Perth	—	—	104
Dunfermline	—	—	50

APPENDIX I

Names of Towns	Year 1789	Year 1791	Year 1815
Arbroath	—	—	75
Brechin	—	—	130
Banff	—	—	136
Elgin	—	—	40
Inverness	—	—	30
Bodmin	—	—	730
Leigh	—	—	436
Grantham	—	—	580
Hexham	—	—	427

APPENDIX II

DIRECTIONS FOR CONGREGATIONAL SINGING

(Issued by John Wesley for the use of the Methodist Societies.)

THAT this part of divine worship may be more acceptable to God, as well as more profitable to yourself and others, be careful to observe the following directions:—

1. Sing *all*. See that you join with the congregation as frequently as you can. Let not a slight degree of weakness or weariness hinder you. If it is a cross to you, take it up, and you will find a blessing.

2. Sing *lustily*, and with a good courage. Beware of singing as if you were half dead, or half asleep; but lift up your voice with strength. Be no more afraid of your voice now, nor more ashamed of it being heard, than when you sung the songs of Satan.

3. Sing *modestly*. Do not bawl, so as to be heard above, or distinct from, the rest of the congregation, that you may not destroy the harmony; but strive to unite your voices together, so as to make one clear melodious sound.

4. Sing *in time*. Whatever time is sung, be sure to keep with it. Do not run before, nor stay behind it; but attend closely to the leading voices, and move therewith as exactly as you can. And take care you sing not too slow. This drawling way naturally steals on all who are lazy; and it is high time to drive it out from among us, and sing all our tunes just as quick as we did at first.

5. Above all, sing *spiritually*. Have an eye to God in every word you sing. Aim at pleasing Him more than yourself, or any other creature. In order to do this, attend strictly to the sense of what you sing; and see that your heart is not carried away with the sound, but offered to God continually; so shall your singing be such as the Lord will approve of here, and reward when He cometh in the clouds of heaven.

BIBLIOGRAPHY

In the list of Contemporary Sources I have tried to indicate, in a few words, books that have any special interest for this subject.

In the list of General Works I have not attempted to assess the importance of any book, but those that have any special bearing on the subject I have indicated by a mark, i.e.* N.D. indicates no date of publication.

LIST OF NEWSPAPERS AND PERIODICALS

Annual Register, 1791–1815.
Anti-Jacobin Review, 1799–1805.
Anti-Slavery Monthly Reporter, 1827–1833. (Useful for part Methodism played in abolition of Slavery.)
Arminian Magazine, 1778–1797. (The official Methodist publication. Useful as index to Methodist religious thought.)
British Critic, 1793–1800.
Catholic Vindicator, 1819. (A counterblast to Protestant periodicals.)
Christian Reformer, 5 vols., 1815–1819. (Paper of the Unitarians.)
Christian Register, 1829.
Critical Review, 1756–1790.
Eclectic Review, 1805–1866.
Edinburgh Review, 1802–1820. (Occasional reference to Methodism and an important article in 1808.)
European Magazine (to 1815).
Evangelical Magazine, 1793–1815. (Many references to religious work of Methodism. Favourable in tone.)
Gentleman's Magazine, 1731–1816. (Invaluable for a study of Methodism in the eighteenth century. Reference to social aspect of Methodism and the writings of John Wesley.)
London Gazette, 1741–1791.
London Quarterly Review, 1853 onward.
Methodist Magazine, 1798–1821. (Continuation of *Arminian Magazine*. No change in style.)
Missionary Notices, 1816–1838. (Useful for work of Methodism in the West Indies.)
Monthly Magazine, 1796–1810.
Monthly Review, 1749–1816. (Together with *Gentleman's Magazine*, is most important periodical for a study of Methodism.)
Oracle, The, 1792.

Quarterly Review, 1809–1820. (Unfavourable to Methodism. Important long article in November 1810.)
Parlour Window, 1795.
Patriot, The, 1792–1793.
Philanthropist, 1795. (A violently democratic publication: extremely daring.)
Political State, 1720–1740. (Some references to George Whitefield: none to John Wesley.)
Protestant Advocate, 1813–1818. (Violently anti-Romanist.)
Protestant Dissenters' Magazine, 1794–1799. (6 vols.)
Protestant Magazine, 1839–1865.
Republican, The, 1819–1826. (14 vols.) (Repeated onslaughts on Methodism as the ally of the governing classes.)
St. James' Chronicle, 1769–1800. Imperfect.
Sunday School Teachers' Magazine, 1830–1843. (14 vols.) (Important for an understanding of methods, hours and subjects in a Sunday School.)
Tracts of Anti-Slavery Society.
Tribune, 1795–1796. (3 vols.) (Radical in tone. Contained democratic lectures of Thelwall.)
Watchman, The, 1845–1850. (Consulted for Chartist agitation because most important Methodist paper for this period. Conservative in tone.)
Wesleyan Methodist Magazine, 1822–1839.
Wesleyan Reformer, 1852.
Wesleyan Spectator, Nos. 1–14, 1863.

LIST OF CONTEMPORARY SOURCES

Agutter, William: *Christian Politics*, 1792; *The Fruitful Soldier and the True Christian*, 1798.
Alexander, Disney: *The Reason of Methodism*. (N.D.)
Allen, R.: *Methodism in Preston*, 1864.
Anderson, James: *Observations on Slavery*, 1789.
Arthur, William, *The Successful Merchant*, 1835 (Methodism in Business); *The American Question*, 1881.
Atmore, Charles: *An Account of Eliza Atmore*, 1794.
Barrett, G.: *Recollections of Methodists in Lincoln*. (Useful local history. Shows slow progress of Methodism in rural areas.)
Batty, J.: *History of Rothwell*, 1877. (Interesting for its references to pew rents.)
Beaumont, L.: *Life of Rev. Joseph Beaumont, M.D.*, 1855.
Benson, J.: *Further Defence of Methodism in Five Letters*, 1794; *Four*

Sermons on the Future Misery of the Wicked. (An element in Methodist preaching of this period.)
Birks, W.: *John Wesley and Methodism.* (N.D.)
Bons, J.: *How to Fill our Churches,* 1885.
Bowdler, John: *Reform or Ruin,* 1823.
Boyce, G.: *A Serious Reply to John Wesley.* (N.D.)
Braithwaite, J.P.: *Memoirs of J. J. Gurney,* 2 vols., 1854.
Bretherton, F. F.: *Early Methodism in and around Chester,* 1903. (A good local history.)
Buck, R. E. E.: *How Wesley's Society lapsed into Schism.*
Bulmer, Agnes: *Memoirs of Mrs. Elizabeth Mortimer.*
Bunting, Jabez: *A Great Work Described,* 1805. (Reference to Sunday-School work.)
Bunting, T. P.: *The Life of Jabez Bunting,* 1859. (A standard work, well documented and most important as a study of the greatest Methodist since Wesley.) *Laymen in Conference,* 1871.
Burdekin, R.: *Memoirs of Mr. R. Spence,* 1837.
Burdsall, John: *Life of R. Burdsall, of York,* 1823.
Burgess, W. P.: *Memoirs of the Rev. J. Burgess,* 1842.
Caine, C.: *History of Wesleyan Methodism in Crewe,* 1883; *Chronicle of Methodism in West Leyton, 1750–1895.*
Carter, W. B.: *Methodism Past and Present,* 1852.
Carus, W.: *Memoirs of the Rev. C. Simeon,* 1847.
Carvosso, W.: Memoirs of, by his Son, 1847.
Chick, E.: *History of Wesleyan Methodism in Exeter, 1739–1907.*
Clapham, S.: *How Far Methodism Conduces to the Interests of Christianity,* 1794; *A Sermon for Charity Schools,* 1792; *Sermon before an Association of Ministers,* 1792.
Clarke, Adam: *The Origin and End of Civil Government,* 1822. (Not an important book, but very useful in showing the political philosophy of a representative leader of Methodism.)
Clarke, Adam: *Memoirs of Mrs. Mary Cooper,* 1818.
Clarkson, T.: *Abolition of the Slave Trade,* 1808. (Warm appreciation of Wesley's support of the Committee for Abolition of Slave Trade.)
Coetlogon, C. E. De: *Peculiar Advantage of the English Nation,* 1792.
Coke and Moore: *Life of John Wesley,* 1839.
Cooke, Jos.: *Genuine Methodism Examined.* (N.D.)
Cooper, Thomas: *Life of Thomas Cooper,* 1897. (An excellent Autobiography. In its early chapters interesting sidelights on Methodism. Specially good for the Chartist period.)
Court, L. A.: *Romance of a Country Circuit.* (N.D.) (Methodism in a difficult area.)
Crookshank, C. H.: *A Methodist Pioneer: Life of J. Smith,* 1881; *Methodism in Ireland,*

Crowther, J.: *The Crisis of Methodism*, 1795. (Democracy inside Methodism.) *Strictures on Petitioning for Preachers among Methodists.*
Cubitt, George: *Observations on Dr. Warren's Pamphlets Against the Wesleyan Institution*, 1834.
Cudworth, W.: *Preservative in Perilous Times*, 1818.
Davis, M.: *Thoughts on Dancing*, 1791
Dixon, R. W.: *A Century of Village Nonconformity*, 1887.
Drew, S.: *Life of the Rev. Thomas Coke*, 1817. (Dull, but the subject is important.)
Du Bois, W. E. B.: *Suppression of the Slave Trade*, 1896.
Dunn, S.: *Life of Adam Clarke*, 1863.
Dyson, J. B.: *Methodism in the Isle of Wight*, 1865; *Methodism in the Congleton Circuit*, 1856.
Egan, Pierce: *Life in London.*
Entwistle, J. O. E.: *Memoirs of*, by his son, 1848.
Etheridge, J. W.: *Life of Adam Clarke*, 1858. (Probably the best book on the subject.) *Life of Thomas Coke*, 1860.
Evans, J.: *Complete Religious Liberty Vindicated*, 1813. (Interesting as showing that Methodism was opposed to full religious liberty because it would include Catholics.)
Everett, J.: *A Subject's Tribute to George III*, 1839; *Life of Adam Clarke*, 3 vols., 1849; *Memoirs of W. Dawson*, 1842; *Memoirs of the Rev. Daniel Isaac*, 1839; *The Wall's End Miner*, 1835; *The Village Blacksmith: Memoirs of S. Hick*, 1831; *Methodism as it is*, 2 vols., 1863; *The Allens of Shiney Row.* (Everett was a prolific and racy writer. *The Wall's End Miner* and *The Allens of Shiney Row* are valuable as studies of Methodism in northern areas.)
Fancourt, W.: *Britons and Fellow Countrymen*, 1792. (Loyalist pamphlet.)
Fletcher, E. C.: *The Methodist Class Meeting*, 1873.
Fletcher, Rev. J.: *Complete Works of.* (Fletcher was Wesley's chief helper and his designated successor.)
Foote, S.: *The Methodist*, a Comedy. (Scurrilous attack on Whitefield.)
Fynes, Richard: *The Miners of Northumberland and Durham*, Blyth, 1873. (Valuable, but not many references to Methodism.)
Gamage, R. S.: *History of the Chartists*, 1854.
Gifford, J.: *Plain Address to People of England*, 1792.
Gisborne, T.: *Duties of the Female Sex*, 1810; *Essay on Several Branches of the Political Struggle*, 1841.
Greville: *Memoirs, 1775–1787.*
Guest, J.: *Relics and Records of Men and Manufactures in or Near Rotherham*, 1866. (Tribute to influence of Methodism in manufacturing areas.)

BIBLIOGRAPHY

Hales, W.: *Methodism Inspected*, Pt. 1, 1803; Pt. 2, 1805. (Pungent attack on Methodism.)
Hargreaves, J.: *Address to the Heads of Families on the Neglect of Family Religion*, 1811; *Life of the Rev. James Hirst*, 1816.
Hatton, W.: *A brief Account of Local Preachers*, 1822.
Hervey, Lord John: *Memoirs of Reign of George II.*
Hillyard, Bailey: *Numerical Statistics of Methodism*, 1849.
Hitchins and Drew: *History of Cornwall*, 2 vols., 1824.
Holyoake, G. J.: *Life of Rayner Stephens*, 1881. (The subject is important because for some years Rayner Stephens was a Methodist Minister.) *Sixty years of an Agitator's Life*, 2 vols., 1892; *The Rich Man's Six and the Poor Man's One Day* (N.D.); *Self Help by People; Life of Richard Carlile*.
Hudson, W.: *Answer to Bishop Wordsworth's Pastoral*, 1873.
Hunt, Leigh: *Attempt to show the Folly and Danger of Methodism*. (A Churchman fears the growing power of Methodism and attacks its emotionalism and other-worldliness.)
Huskisson Papers, 1792–1830.
Ingram, R. A.: *Causes of the Increase of Methodism*, 1807.
Jackson, T.: *The Conduct of John Wesley in Regard to the Church of England*, 1834; *The Church and Methodists*, 1834; *Recollections of My Life and Times*, 1873. (An interesting commentary on the Methodism of his day, also his early education.) *Lives of Early Methodist Preachers*, 6 vols.
Jennings, L. J.: *Crocker's Correspondence and Diaries, 1800–1830.*
Jessop, W.: *Methodism in Rossendale*, 1880.
Johnson, R. Brimley: *Letters of Hannah More*.
Jones, John: *The Reason of Man*, 1793.
Kelly, H.: *Impartial History of Independent Methodism in Northumberland and Durham*, 1824. (Important in showing that some Methodists were Reformers.)
Lackington, James: *Memoirs of*, 1791. (Although a Methodist for some years, his tone is unfriendly to Methodism.)
Lester, George: *The Wesleys in Lincolnshire*, 1890; *Grimsby Methodism*.
Lyth, John, D.D.: *Glimpses of Early Methodism in York*, 1885. (One of the most important of all the local histories. Particularly useful in showing how Methodists helped Wilberforce.)
Macdonald, F. W.: *Letters of J. Macdonald with Notes* (1816–1831), edited by.
Macdonald, G. B.: *Facts against Fiction*, 1832.
Mallinson, Joel: *History of Methodism in Huddersfield*, 1898.
Martineau, Harriet: *Introduction to the History of Peace*.
Milburn, M. M.: *Letters to Wesleyan Methodists* (N.D.)
Minutes of Wesleyan Conference, 1744 to Date.

McAllum, D.: *Memoirs of the Rev. H. Taft*, 1824.
Moore, H.: *Society and Manners in France*, 1800, 2 vols.
Moore, H.: *Fear God, Honour the King*, 1794. (Strongly loyalist.)
More, Hannah: *Complete Works of.*
Morrison, Ambrose: *Letter to Mr. J. McGregor*, 1819.
Newton, J.: *The Imminent Danger and only sane Resource of this Nation*, 1794.
Nightingale, J.: *Portraiture of Methodism*, 1807. (Unfriendly.)
O'Leary, A.: *Remarks on Letter and Defence of Protestant Association by John Wesley*. (The clever attacks of an Irish priest on the bigotry of John Wesley.)
Osborn, G., D.D.: *Poetical Works of John and Charles Wesley.*
Overton, J.: *The True Churchman Ascertained*, 1802.
Owen, T. E.: *Hints to Heads of Families*, 1802; *Methodism Unmasked*, 1802. (A Churchman attacks Methodism.)
Packer, George: *Centenary of M.N.C.*, 1897.
Parsons, Edward: *The True Patriot: A Letter to the Rev. Author of a Candid Inquiry into the Democratic Schemes of Dissenters*, 1801. (Says Dissenters are not agitators but perfectly loyal.)
Pawlyn, J. S.: *Bristol Methodism.* (Excellent local history.)
Pawson, John: Life and Sermons of, 1801.
Phillips, H.: Memoirs of, 1821.
Pilkington, W.: *Makers of Wesleyan Methodism in Preston*, 1890. (A readable account of Methodism in Preston and district.)
Place, Francis: Life of.
Pocock, W. W.: *History of Wesleyan Methodism in some of the Southern Counties*, 1885. (Excellent. Shows the way Methodism failed to grip the southern counties.)
Pratt, A. C.: *Black Country Methodism*, 1891.
Prentice, Archibald: *Historical Sketches of Manchester between 1792 and 1832*; *History of Anti-Corn Law League*, 1853.
Prince, J. H.: *The Christian Duty to God and the Constitution*, 1804. (Loyalist pamphlet.)
Reed, H. B.: *Appeal to Wesleyans*, 1875.
Renshaw, J.: *Memoir of Life and Death of Rebecca Lomas*, 1811.
Rhodes, B.: *Sketch of Constitution of England*, 1795.
Riles, John: *Journal of Samuel Plummer*, 1821.
Roberts, W.: *Memoirs of Hannah More*, 4 vols. (Important, because Hannah More was a leading Evangelical.)
Robinson, Mark: *Observations on the System of Wesleyan Methodism*, 1825.
Robinson, W.: *The Sin of Conformity*, 1863.
Rodda, R.: *Account of Mr. George Ball*, 1809.
Rowland, Thomas: *Letter to James Heald, Esq., M.P.*, 1847; *Memoirs of Isaac Bradnock*, 1835.

BIBLIOGRAPHY

Rule, W. H.: *Wesleyan Methodism in the British Army*, 1883. (Not good, but discusses an important aspect of Methodist work.)
Sandwith, H.: *A Reply to Lord John Russell's Animadversions*, 1830.
Senior, L. M.: *People in our Circuit*, 1887.
Shaw, T.: *Letter to Mr. Benson*, 1797.
Shephard, T.: *Letter to Mr. Richard Carlile*, 1825.
Smith, B.: *History of Methodism in Macclesfield*, 1875.
Smith, George: *History of Methodism*, 3 vols., 1857. (Out of date, but still important.) *Doctrine of the Pastorate*, 1851; *Wesleyan Ministers and their Slanderers*, 1849; *Polity of Wesleyan Methodism*, 1851.
Smith, J.: *History of Liverpool*, 1810. (References to Methodist philanthropy.)
Smith, R.: *Life of Rev. Henry Moore*, 1844; *Memorial Sketches of Robert Carr Brackenbury*, 1859.
Smith, W.: *Letter to William Wilberforce on the Abolition of the Slave Trade*, 1807.
Southey, R.: *Life of John Wesley*. (The best life from a literary point of view.)
Stamp, W. W.: *Methodism in Bradford*, 1841; *The Orphan House of Wesley*, 1863.
Steele, A.: *Methodism in Barnard Castle*, 1857; *Methodism in Earnest: Life of the Rev. H. Casson*, 1853.
Stephen, James: *Slavery of the West Indian Colonies*, 2 vols., 1830.
Stephens, John: *Sermon preached for Strangers' Friend Society; Sermon Adapted to the State of the Times*, 1829.
Stephens, J. R.: *The Political Preacher*, 1839.
Stevens, Abel: *History of Methodism*, 3 vols. (1858, 1862, 1875). (One of the very best histories of Methodism. Much material and usually quite trustworthy.)
Strachan, Alex.: *Recollections of Life and Times of Rev. George Lowe*, 1848.
Sutcliffe, Jos.: *Review of Methodism*, 1805.
Symons, W.: *Early Methodism in West Somerset*. (N.D.)
Taylor, George: *Letter to W. B. Carter*, 1852.
Taylor, Thomas: *Answer to First Part of 'Age of Reason,'* 1796.
Thomas, J. W.: *Reminiscences of Methodism in Exeter*. (N.D.) (Excellent for effect of Sidmouth's Bill on Methodism.)
Told, Silas: The Life of, by himself, 1796.
Treffry, Richard: *Memoirs of the Rev. Joseph Benson*, 1840.
Treffry, Richard, Junr.: *Memoirs of Mr. J. E. Tresize*, 1837; *Memoirs of Rev. John Smith*, 1833.
Tuck, Stephen: *Wesleyan Methodism in Frome*, 1837.
Tucker, Josiah: *A Brief History of the Principles of Methodism*, 1742.

Turner, D.: *An Exhortation to Support of Government*, 1792. (Loyalist pamphlet.)
Turner, P. C.: *Memoir of T. M. Haswell*, 1843; *Memoirs of Miss Sarah Broster*, 1839.
Tyerman, L.: *Wesley's Designated Successor; Life and Times of John Wesley*. (Not always accurate, but very rich in material. One of the best lives and perhaps the most interesting.)
Vevers, William: *A defence of the Discipline of Methodism*, 1835; *The People's Rights*, 1850; *Wesleyan Methodism Vindicated*, 1847.
Waddy, S. D.: *Life of*, by his youngest daughter, 1878.
Wainwright, Latham: *Observations on the Doctrine and Manners of Wesleyan Methodists*, 1818.
Ward, J.: *Historical Sketches of Methodism in Bingley*, 1863.
Ward, Valentine: *Memoir of the late Rev. J. Nelson*, 1831; *Observations on Sunday Schools*, 1827. (A cogently written argument against writing in Sunday Schools.)
Warren, S.: *Chronicles of Methodism*, 1827.
Watmough, A.: *History of Methodism in Great Yarmouth*, 1826; *History of Methodism in Lincoln*, 1829.
Watson, H. (Bishop of Llandaff): *Address to the People of Great Britain*, 1798; *Sermon preached before Society for Suppression of Vice*, 1804.
Watson, R.: *Complete Works of*. (Shows Watson's enthusiasm for abolition of Slavery.)
Watts, I.: *The Improvement of the Mind*, 1809.
Welch, Charles: *The Wesleyan Crisis*, 1835.
Wenderborn, F. A.: *A View of England Towards the Close of the Eighteenth Century*, 1791. (Valuable for social history.)
Wesley, John: *Complete Works of*, 14 vols.; *Journals, Standard*, 8 vols.; *Letters, Standard*, 8 vols. (Indispensable.)
West, F. A.: *Memoirs of Mrs. J. Gibson*, 1837.
West, George: *Methodism in Marshland*, 1886.
West, R. A.: *Sermons of W. Dawson*, 1860. (Instructive as showing the subjects preached on by a popular preacher.)
White, J. B.: *Poor Man's Preservative against Popery*, 1829. (Anti-Catholic, but slight in value.)
Wilberforce, William: *Practical View of Prevailing Religious Systems Contrasted with Real Christianity; Correspondence of*.
Wilson, T.: *Dissenting Churches in London*, 4 vols. (The best book on the subject.)
Wood, J.: *Directions to Class Leaders*, 1812.
Wood, Thomas: *Essays on Civil Government*, 1796. (Strongly loyalist.) *Sketch of Mr. James Bundy*. (N.D.)
Young, A.: *Enquiry into State of Mind among the Lower Classes*, 1798.

ANONYMOUS

'A Cool Reply to "the Calm Address." '
'Account of General Baptisms by a Mechanic' 1795.
'Affectionate Address to Methodists by Onesimus.' (N.D.)
'A New Year's Gift to Wesleyan Methodism,' 1822. (A most trenchant attack on Methodism.)
'A New Pair of Scales,' 1806.
'An Answer to the Question "Why are you a Wesleyan Methodist?" ' 1842.
'Anti-Sectarian,' 1834.
'Apology for M.N.C. by a Trustee and a Layman,' 1813. (Protest against autocracy of Conference.)
'Concise Sketch of an Intended Revolution in England,' 1794.
'Condemner of Methodism Condemned,' 1814.
'Confessions of a Methodist,' by a Professor, 1810. (A wittily-written account of the growing prosperity of Methodism and the imposition of Pew Rents.)
'Controversial Tracts on Tractarians,' 1842.
'Defence of Alexander Kilham at his Trial,' 1796. (Protest against despotism of Conference.)
'Defence of the Wesleyan Theological Institution,' 1834.
'Dialogue between a Methodist Preacher and a Minister of the Church of England,' 1778.
'Ecclesiastical Principles of Wesleyan Methodism in Relation to existing Religious and Political Parties,' 1841.
'Facts, Reflections, and Queries,' 1792.
'Few Words on the Increase of Methodism,' 1810.
'Guilt of the Democratic Scheming fully Proved,' by the Inquirer, 1802. (Attack on the loyalty of Dissenters.)
'History and Rules of Calvinistic Methodists,' 1840.
'Letter to a Country Gentleman on Methodism,' 1805.
'Letter to a Friend wherein Mr. Paine's Letter to Mr. Dundas is considered,' 1792.
'Letter of Committee, appointed by General Baptist Assembly.' (N.D.)
'Letter to John Wesley,' 1778.
'Letter to the Treasurer of Society for the Abolition of the Slave Trade by the Rev. Robert B. Nicholls,' 1788.
'Liberty and Equality Treated in a Short History Addressed from a Poor Man to his Equals,' 1792.
'List of Society instituted in 1787 for Effecting the Abolition of Slave Trade,' 1787.
'Memoirs of Members of M.N.C. Mossley Circuit,' 1839.
'Methodism: her Bane and Antidote,' by Veritas.

'Methodistical Inconsistency,' 1814.
'Methodism and the Masses,' by a Minister's Wife, 1858.
'Methodism Displayed at London,' 1756.
'Methodism Displayed and Enthusiasm Detected,' 1756.
'Methodism Vindicated from the Charge of Ignorance,' by a Member of the Church of England, 1795.
'Modern Methodism not in Accordance with the Plans of John Wesley,' 1842.
'Modern Wesleyanism Contrasted with the Teaching of John Wesley,' (N.D.)
'Narrative of Methodists Regarding Sidmouth's Bill,' 1811.
'Opinions of Meeting for Signing Declaration of Support of Government,' 1793.
'Political Empiricism, A Letter to John Wesley,' 1776.
'Present Political State of Great Britain,' 1758.
'Principles of Order and Happiness under the British Constitution between a Parish Clerk and Squire,' 1792.
'Principles and Practices of Methodists considered in a Letter to the Rev. G. Whitefield,' 1761.
'Progress of Methodism in the West Indies,' 1805. (Methodism strong among Slave population in W. Indies.)
'Reasons for Leaving the Methodist Society,' 1777.
'Reasons for Methodism in a Letter to the Bishop of Exeter,' 1834.
'Reflections on the Present System of Methodism,' 1824.
'Religion Run Wild.' Examined by Obadiah, 1811.
'Remarks on Priestley's System of Materialism and Mechanism and Necessity in a Series of Letters to Mr. Wesley.' (N.D.)
'Reply to the Affectionate Address of Rev. Rd. Watson,' 1829. (Attack on the Conservatism of Methodism.)
'Rise and Progress of Wesleyan Methodism,' 1831.
'Short Account of Mr. Dillon,' 1817.
'Six Letters to the Right Honourable C. Grant by Simplicius,' 1820.
'Sound an Alarm,' 1798. (Loyalist pamphlet.)
'Speeches in Support of Wesleyan Methodist Association at Darlington,' 1836.
'Strictures on Methodism,' by a Careful Observer, 1804.
'Temporal Prosperity and Spiritual Decline,' by a Wesleyan Minister, 1866.
'The Anti-Levelling Songster,' 1793.
'The Methodist Memorial,' 1871.
'The Principles of Methodists, Ipswich,' 1805.
'The Rise, Progress, and Influence of Wesleyan Methodism,' 1831.
'Visions of Sapience,' 1819.

'Whig Radicalism Against Wesleyan Methodism,' 1841. (Bitter attack on Popery and Liberalism.)
'Wrongs of Man,' by a Patriot, 1792.

COLLECTED PAMPHLETS AND TRACTS

Cathercole Collection, U.V. (Brit. Mus. 908, e. 4).
Constitution Tracts, 8135, b. 23.
Early Methodist Tracts (Seven Pamphlets mainly on Whitefield).
Irish Broadsides (96 odd Pamphlets between 1679 and 1756).
Letters: Addresses for Dublin, 1749–1761.
Miscellaneous Tracts (Brit. Mus. 10347 d. e. 48), 1768–1799.
Pamphlets (Brit, Mus. 4257, f. 47), 5 Tracts.
Parliamentary Debates, 1804–1813 (W. Cobbett); 1813–1820 (Hansard).
Political Tracts (Brit. Mus. 8139, d. f. 17), 13 Pamphlets, 1798–1812.
Politics (12 Tracts), 1767–1768.
Political Tracts, 1819. Newcastle, 8135, c. 2.
Politics for the people, 1794.
Proceedings of Wesley Historical Society. Complete.
Public Record Office:—State Papers, Domestic, George III. (1811.)
Religious Biography (Brit. Mus. 4920, b. 55), 7 Memoirs, 1710–1860.
Religious and Ecclesiastical Tracts (Brit. Mus. 10347, c. 29), 1831–1848.
Sermons (Brit. Mus. Collection), 1781–1845.
Sermons, 4473, bb. 9. 1799–1844.
Sermons (12), 4473, f. 2.
Sermons on Important Subjects by Wesleyan Methodist Ministers, 1832.
Theological Tracts, 1792–1896 (4371, bb. 24), 9 Tracts.
Tracts on Dissent (14), 4136, c. 1.
Tracts on Dissent (25), 4136, c. 3.
Tracts on Dissent (14), 4136, de. 1.
Tracts on Dissent (Brit. Mus. 4136, e. 2), 16 Tracts, 1790–1809.
Tracts on Dissent (Brit. Mus. 4139, b. 1), 29 Tracts.
Tracts on Dissent (Brit. Mus. 4135, c. 2), 1811–1835.
Tracts on Dissenters (5), 4136, aa, 77.
Tracts relating to Dissenters (Brit. Mus. 4139, c. 2), 9 Tracts.
Tracts on Slavery, 1792–1807. 10 Tracts.
Tracts on Slavery, 1773–1829. 13 Tracts. (Preserved in Friends' Meeting House.)
Tracts on Education, including Lecture on Religious Education by W. N. Molesworth, 1849.
Wesleyan Methodist Sermons, London, 1832.
Wesleyan Tracts (Brit. Mus. 4136, c. 9), 3 Pamphlets, 1795–1837.
Wesleyan Tracts (Brit. Mus. 4136, c. 10), 28 Pamphlets.

Wesleyan Tracts (Brit. Mus. 4136, c. 8), 20 Pamphlets, 1777–1832.
Wesleyan Tracts (Brit. Mus. 4136, c. 11), 27 Pamphlets, 1805–1812.
Wesleyan Tracts (Brit. Mus. 4136, c. 7), 38 Pamphlets, 1759–1831.
Wesleyan Tracts (Brit. Mus. 4136, c. 12), 22 Pamphlets, 1792–1807.

LIST OF GENERAL WORKS

Abbey, C. J.: *The English Church and its Bishops*, 1887.
Adamson, J. W.: *English Education, 1789–1902*.
Amherst, W. J.: *History of Roman Catholic Emancipation*.
Bald, M. A.: *Women Writers in the Nineteenth Century*.
Beer, Max: *History of British Socialism*, Vol. I, 1919; *History of British Socialism*, Vol. II, 1920.
Bett, Henry: *The Hymns of Methodism in their Literary Relations*.
Binns, Elliott: *The Evangelical Movement*.
Birley: *English Jacobins, 1789–1802*.
Brash, W. B.: *Methodism*.
Brinton, Crane: *The Political Ideas of the English Romanticists*, 1926.
*Brown, P. H.: *The French Revolution in English History*.
Burt, Thomas.: *An Autobiography*, 1924.
Chapman, E. M.: *English Literature and Religion*.
Cobban, Alf.: *Edmund Burke and the Revolt against the Eighteenth Century*, 1929.
Cole, G. D. H.: *Robert Owen; Short History of the British Working Class Movement; William Cobbett*.
Colligan, J. H.: *The Arian Movement in England*, 1913; *Nonconformity in the Eighteenth Century*, 1915.
Colquhoun, J. C.: *Wilberforce and his Friends*.
*Coupland, R.: *William Wilberforce, A Narrative*.
*Cruse, Amy.: *The Englishman and his Books in the Nineteenth Century*.
Davis, H. W. C.: *Age of Grey and Peel*, 1929.
Dent, R. K.: *The Making of Birmingham*.
Dicey, A. V.: *The Statesmanship of Wordsworth*, 1917; *Law and Opinion in England*.
Dimond, S. C.: *The Psychology of the Methodist Revival*.
Dobbs, A. E.: *Educational and Social Movements in England, 1700–1850*.
Drinkwater, John: *Life of C. J. Fox*.
Eayrs, G.: *Wesley and Kingswood; Wesley, Christian Philosopher and Church Founder*.
Eden, F. M.: *The State of the Poor*.
*Fay, C. R.: *Life and Labour in the Nineteenth Century; Great Britain from Adam Smith to the present Day*.
*Faulkner, H. V.: *Chartism and the Churches*, 1916; New York.

BIBLIOGRAPHY

Faulkner, J. A.: *Wesley as a Sociologist.*
Fausset, H. I.: *Life of S. T. Coleridge; Life of W. Cowper,* 1928.
Findlay, G. G., and Holdsworth, W. W.: *History of Wesleyan Methodist Missionary Society;* Vol. IV. (Fine account of Methodist work in the West Indies.)
*Freemantle, A. F.: *England in the Nineteenth Century.*
George, M. D.: *England in Transition; English Social Life in the Eighteenth Century; London Life in the Eighteenth Century.*
Gibbons, H. De S.: *English Social Reformers; Industrial History of England.*
Gill, Conrad: *The Naval Mutinies of 1797* (1913).
Glover, Arnold: *Boswell's Johnson,* 3 vols.
Gounelle, E.: *Wesley et ses Rapports avec les Français.*
Guest, Richard: *Compendious History of Cotton Manufacturers.*
*Halévy, E.: *History of the English People in 1815; The Growth of Philosophic Radicalism.*
Hammond, J. L. and B.: *Rise of Modern Industry; The Town Labourer, 1760–1832; The Village Labourer, 1760–1832; The Skilled Labourer, 1760–1832; The Age of the Chartists.*
*Hearnshaw, F. C.: *The Social and Political Ideas of some Representative Thinkers of the Revolutionary Era.* Edited by.
*Holt, Ann: *Life of Joseph Priestley.*
Hunt, J.: *Religious Thought in England in the Nineteenth Century.*
Hutchins, B. L., and Harrison, D.: *History of Factory Legislation.*
Iceley, H. E. M.: *English History from Contemporary Sources.*
Jephson, Henry: *The Platform,* 1896.
*Klingberg, F. S.: *The Anti-slavery Movement in England.*
Kent, C. B. R.: *The English Radicals,* 1899.
Lascelles, E.: *Granville Sharpe.*
Laycock, J. W.: *Methodist Heroes in the Great Haworth Round,* 1909.
Lecky, W. E. E.: *England in the Eighteenth Century.*
Leger, A.: *L'Angleterre Religieuse.*
Lelievre, M.; *Wesley, his Life and Work.*
Lunn, Arnold: *John Wesley.*
Maccoby, Simon: *Eighteenth Century England.*
Marshall, Dorothy: *The English Poor in the Eighteenth Century.*
Marin, R. E.: *The Anti-slavery Movement in Kentucky.*
McGiffert, A. C.: *Protestant Thought before Kant.*
Meakin, Annette: *Hannah More.*
Merz, J. T.: *History of European Thought.*
Milner, Mary: *Life of Dean Milner.*
Morgan, R. B.: *Readers in English Social History.*
Mowat, R. B.: *England in the Eighteenth Century.*

McLachlan, H.: *English Education under the Test Acts*, 1931.
Newman, Sir George: *Health and Social Evolution.*
*North, E. M.: *Early Methodist Philanthropy*, 1914.
Overton, J. H.: *Life in the English Church, 1660–1714.*
Overton, J. H., and Relton, F.: *History of the Church of England.*
*Overton, J. H.: *Evangelical Revival in the Eighteenth Century.*
Overton, J. H., and Abbey, C. J.: *The English Church in the Eighteenth Century.*
Parker, Irene: *Dissenting Academies in England.*
*Parkinson, George: *True Stories of Durham Pit Life*, 1912.
Paston, George: *Little Memoirs of the Eighteenth Century.*
Pattison, A. S. P.: *The Philosophic Radicals*, 1907.
Patterson, M. W.: *Sir Francis Burdett*, 2 vols, *Northern Primitive Methodism*, 1909.
*Pellew, G.: *Life of Lord Sidmouth*, 3 vols.
*Piette, Maximin: *La Réaction Wesleyenne dans l'évolution Protestant.*
Pinchbeck, Ivy: *Women Workers in the Industrial Revolution.*
Prince, J. W.: *Wesleyan Religious Education.*
Rattenbury, Owen: *Flame of Freedom*, 1931.
Rattenbury, J. E.: *Wesley's Legacy to the World.*
Richardson, A. E.: *Georgian England.*
Rigg, J. H.: *The Living Wesley.*
Roscoe, E. S.: *The English Scene in the Eighteenth Century.*
Rosenblatt, Frank: *The Chartist Movement.*
Rose, J. H.: *Life of William Pitt; The Revolutionary and Napoleonic Era, 1780–1815.*
Sichel, W.: *The Glenbervie Journals*, edited by.
*Simon J. S.: *John Wesley and the Methodist Societies; John Wesley and the Religious Societies; John Wesley and the Advance of Methodism; John Wesley the Master Builder; John Wesley and the Last Phase; Revival in England in the Eighteenth Century.*
Smart, W.: *Economic Annals in the Nineteenth Century, 1801–1820.*
Smith, F.: *Life of Sir J. Kay Shuttleworth*, 1923.
Smith, W. M. Henry: *Political History of Slavery.*
Somervell, D. C.: *English Thought in the Nineteenth Century.*
Stephen, J.: *Essays in Ecclesiastical Biography.*
Stephen, Leslie: *English Thought in the Eighteenth Century*, 1876; *The English Utilitarians*, 1900.
Stoughton, J.: *History of Religion in England.*
*Tawney, R. H.: *Religion and the Rise of Capitalism.*
*Telford, J.: *Life of John Wesley; Life of Charles Wesley; Wesley's Chapel and Wesley's House.*
Thomas, Rowland: *Richard Price.*
Traill, H. D.: *Social England*, Vol. V.

Trevelyan, G. M.: *British History in the Nineteenth Century; Early History of C. J. Fox.*
Tullock, John: *Movements of Religious Thought in Britain,* 1885.
Turberville, A. S.: *Men and Manners in the Eighteenth Century.*
*Veitch, G. S.: *The Genesis of Parliamentary Reform.*
Vulliamy, C. E.: *Life of John Wesley.*
Wale, W.: *Journals of George Whitefield.*
Walker, J. W.: *Methodism in Maidenhead,* 1919.
Wallas, G.: *Life of Francis Place.*
*Warner, W. J.: *The Wesleyan Movement in the Industrial Revolution.*
Webb, S. and B.: *English Local Government,* Vols. VIII and IX.
*Webb, Sidney: *The Story of the Durham Miners,* 1921.
*Weber, Max: *The Protestant Ethic and the Spirit of Capitalism,* 1931.
*Welbourne, E.: *Miners' Union of Northumberland and Durham,* 1923, Cambridge.
Wilberforce, R. I. and S. W.: *Life of William Wilberforce.*
Wilson, John: *History of Durham Miners' Association,* 1907; *Memoirs of a Labour Leader,* 1910.
Workman, H. B.: *Methodism.*
*Workman, H. B., Eayrs, G., and Townsend, W. J.: *New History of Methodism,* 2 vols.
Wyndham, Maud: *Chronicles of the Eighteenth Century.*

INDEX

Aristocracy, 133, 134, 145, 146

Beaumont, Joseph, 158
Benevolent Societies, 117
Benezet, Anthony, 64
Benson, Joseph, 29, 48, 58, 90, 91, 123
Bentham, 41
Benthamism, 41, 115
Bible Christians, 51, 52, 53
Book Room, 129
Bourne, Hugh, 53, 55
Bradburn, Samuel, 58
Bunting, Jabez :
  His Politics, 155–6
  His Preaching, 153–4
  His Youth, 151
  Opponents, 156–61
  Organizing Ability, 151, 153
  Relations with Luddites, 30–1
  Relations with Reformers, 35, 36, 91
  Relations with Roman Catholics, 115
  Relations with Slave Traffic, 71
  Services to Education, 154
  Work for Missionary Society, 153
Burt, Thomas, 108
Butterworth, Joseph, 78, 92, 114, 115, 123

Calvin, 86
Carlile, Richard, 29, 78, 92, 102, 115, 145, 146
Charity Schools, 103
Chartism, 37, 56
Clapham Sect, 123
Clarke, Adam, 18, 28, 77, 78, 123, 129

Clarkson, Thomas, 66
Class Meetings, 45
Clowes, Wm., 54, 55
Cobbett, Wm., 24, 25, 32
Coke, Thomas, 70, 77, 129, 151, 152
Cooper, Thomas, 56

Dames' Schools, 103
Dancing, 128
Dispensaries, 117
Dissenters, 25, 26, 27, 28
Dissenting Academies, 102, 103
Distribution of Methodism, 141–5
Dress, 134
Durham, 107

Education, Part III, Chapter 2
Elliott, Ebenezer, 92
Evangelicals, 119–24
Everett, James, 158, 159, 160

Farmers, 143, 144
Fletcher (of Madeley), 15, 120
Flysheet Agitation, 158–61
Fowler, Joseph, 158
Fox, George, 40, 63, 68
French Revolution, 21

Gambling, 133–4
Grammar Schools, 102
Grimshaw of Haworth, 120

Haircutting, 136
Harris, Howel, 142
Health and Morals Act, 119
Hobbes, 42
Holland, Lord, 78
Hymn Book of Methodism, 43, 44

Increase of Methodism, 141
Independent Methodists, 59
Industrial Revolution, Part III, Chapter 1
Industry—Schools of, 103
Ireland, 142
Isaac, Daniel, 35, 69

Junius, 19

Kilham, Alexander, 48, 49, 50, 51, 52, 53
Kingswood School, 100

Labourers, 143-4
Leeds, Brunswick, 157
Lending Stock, 118
Liverpool, Lord, 78, 80
Locke, 17, 40
Luddites, 29, 30, 31

Macaulay, T. B., 71
Methodism :
   Charges of Disloyalty, 24
   Despotism of Government, 47, 48, 92
   Economic Viewpoint, 95-9
   Love of the Constitution, 28, 41, 149, 150
   Preaching, 24, 25
   Reform Agitation in the North, 32-6
   Relations with R.C.'s, 114
   Sidmouth's Bill, 75-82
   Slave Trade Agitation, 68-71
   Social Life, 127-38
Missionaries, 70, 71, 73, 74
Monthly Reviews, 65
Music, 130, 131
Mutinies at Spithead and the Nore, 21

Napoleonic War, 148-50

Oastler, Richard, 98, 116
O'Bryan, William, 51, 52, 53
O'Leary, Father, 112

Old Testament, 18
Open Air Speaking, 45

Paine, Thomas, 21, 29, 48
Perceval, 79
Perronet, Vincent, 120
Peterloo Massacre, 33-4, 58, 75
Petrie, John, 158
Pew Rents, 22, 90, 91
Political Thought of Methodism, 16 f.
Presbyterianism, 27, 142
Price (Dr.), 27
Priestley, Joseph (Dr.), 27
Primitive Methodism—*see* Hugh Bourne, 93
Psalms, 86
Public Schools, 102

Quakers, 39, 40, 63

Renaissance, 41, 42
Reformation, 38, 86
Rousseau, 17, 40

Sadler, Michael, 116
Scriptural Holiness, 22, 23, 24, 38
Sharpe, Granville, 66
Shuttleworth, Kay, 101
Sidmouth, Viscount, 75-9
Simeon, 122
Smoking, 128
Smuggling, 118-19
Snuff-taking, 128
Southey, R., 75
Spirituous Liquors, 131-3
Sports, 134
Steele, James, 54
Stephens, John, 35, 58, 91
Stephens, J. Rayner, 56
Sunday Observance, 136-7
Sunday Schools, 102-9

Theatres, 127, 128-9
Thompson, Thomas, 92, 123
Tolpuddle Martyrs, 35, 92, 155

INDEX

Trustees, 15, 90
Tyneside, 36, 57, 58

Vessels decoyed, 118–19

Wales, 142
War of American Independence, 19, 27
Warren, Samuel, 156, 157
Watson, Richard, 69, 71, 72, 73, 74
Watts, Isaac, 86
Wealth of Methodist Society, 21, 22
Wesley, Charles, 43 ff., 86, 87, 121, 122
Whitefield, George, 64, 111
Wilberforce, 66–9, 123
Wilkes, 19
Wesley, John :
   French Revolution, 21, 29
   Organizing Powers, 15

His Economic Individualism, 94, 95
His Influence on Methodism, 20–21
His Political Proposals, 20
His Relations with Church of England, 25, 121
His Relations with Dissenters, 26
His Sermons, 22, 24
His Teaching on Holiness, 22
His Toryism, 16, 17
His Views on Business, 89, 90
His Views on Education, 100
His Views on Money, 95–7
His Views on the Poor, 117
His Views on Roman Catholics, 114
His Views on Slavery, 65, 66, 67
His Views on Social Life, 127–38
His Views on Stewardship, 97
His Views on Wilkes and Junius, 19

www.ingramcontent.com/pod-product-compliance
Lightning Source LLC
Chambersburg PA
CBHW050804160426
43192CB00010B/1632